MASTERING LINUX:

FROM ZERO TO RHCSA

BY

O.H. SAMME

Chapter 1:

Introduction to Linux and the RHCSA Certification

- ❖ History and philosophy of Linux
- ❖ Overview of Red Hat Enterprise Linux (RHEL)
- ❖ RHCSA certification: requirements and benefits
- ❖ Setting up a learning environment

Chapter 2:

Basic Linux Commands and File System Navigation

- ❖ Command-line interface basics
- ❖ File system hierarchy standard
- ❖ Essential commands for file and directory manipulation
- ❖ Understanding file permissions and ownership

Chapter 3:

User and Group Management

- ❖ Creating and managing user accounts
- ❖ Group administration
- ❖ Password policies and user security
- ❖ Configuring sudo access

Chapter 4:

Storage Management and File Systems

- ❖ Partitioning and formatting disks
- ❖ Managing LVM (Logical Volume Management)
- ❖ Creating and mounting file systems
- ❖ Implementing disk quotas

Chapter 5:

Process and Service Management

- ❖ Understanding Linux processes
- ❖ Monitoring system resources
- ❖ Managing services with systemd
- ❖ Configuring system startup and shutdown procedures

Chapter 6:

Networking Fundamentals

- ❖ TCP/IP basics
- ❖ Configuring network interfaces
- ❖ DNS and hostname resolution
- ❖ Troubleshooting network issues

Chapter 7:

Package Management and Software Installation

❖ Using YUM and DNF package managers
❖ Managing software repositories
❖ Installing, updating, and removing packages
❖ Compiling software from source

Chapter 8:

System Security and Access Control

❖ Implementing firewalls with firewalld
❖ SELinux basics and configuration
❖ Securing SSH access
❖ Auditing system security

Chapter 9:

System Monitoring and Logging

❖ Configuring system logging
❖ Analyzing log files
❖ Monitoring system performance
❖ Creating and managing cron jobs

Chapter 10:

Backup, Recovery, and System Maintenance

- ❖ Implementing backup strategies
- ❖ Restoring from backups
- ❖ Updating and patching systems
- ❖ Troubleshooting boot issues

Introduction

In an age where technology permeates every aspect of our lives, the demand for skilled professionals who can navigate and manage complex computer systems has never been higher. At the heart of this technological revolution lies Linux, an open-source operating system that powers everything from smartphones to supercomputers. But for many, Linux remains an enigma—a powerful tool shrouded in mystery and technical jargon. This is where "Mastering Linux: From Zero to RHCSA" steps in, offering a comprehensive guide to demystify Linux and equipping you with the skills needed to become a certified Red Hat System Administrator.

Linux, born from the vision of Linus Torvalds in 1991, has grown from a hobbyist project to a cornerstone of modern computing. Its philosophy of openness, collaboration, and continuous improvement has not only shaped the software itself but has also fostered a global community of developers and users. Today, Linux powers the majority of the world's servers, underpins the Android operating system, and forms the backbone of cloud computing infrastructure. Understanding Linux is no longer a niche skill; it's a fundamental requirement for anyone looking to thrive in the digital age.

This book takes a unique approach to learning Linux by focusing on Red Hat Enterprise Linux (RHEL), one of the most popular and widely used distributions in enterprise environments. RHEL's stability, security features, and extensive support make it the go-to choice for organizations ranging from small businesses to Fortune 500 companies. By mastering RHEL, you're not just learning Linux—you're gaining expertise in a platform that powers mission-critical systems across the globe.

What sets "Mastering Linux: From Zero to RHCSA" apart is its holistic approach to learning. Rather than bombarding you with disconnected facts and commands, this book takes you on a journey from the very basics of Linux to the advanced skills required for the Red Hat Certified System Administrator (RHCSA) certification. Each chapter builds upon the previous one, creating a solid foundation of knowledge that grows organically as you progress through the book. This structured approach ensures that you not only learn the "how" but also understand the "why" behind each concept and command.

The book covers five key themes that are essential for any aspiring Linux administrator. First, it delves into the core principles of Linux, including its history, philosophy, and the fundamental concepts that underpin its design. Understanding these basics is crucial for grasping the more advanced topics that follow. Second, the book focuses on system administration essentials, covering everything from basic command-line navigation to advanced user and group management. These skills form the backbone of day-to-day Linux administration and are indispensable for anyone working with Linux systems.

Third, the book explores the intricacies of Linux networking, teaching you how to configure and troubleshoot network interfaces, understand TCP/IP basics, and resolve DNS issues. In today's interconnected world, these networking skills are vital for managing both local systems and cloud-based infrastructure. Fourth, the book delves into system security, covering topics such as firewall configuration, SELinux, and secure SSH access. With cyber threats on the rise, understanding how to secure Linux systems is more important than ever.

Lastly, the book covers advanced topics such as storage management, process control, and system monitoring. These skills are crucial for optimizing system performance, troubleshooting issues, and ensuring the smooth operation of Linux environments. By mastering these five key themes, you'll be well-equipped to handle a wide range of Linux administration tasks and challenges.

"Mastering Linux: From Zero to RHCSA" is designed for a diverse audience. Whether you're a complete beginner looking to break into the world of

Linux, an IT professional seeking to expand your skill set, or an aspiring system administrator aiming for RHCSA certification, this book has something for you. The step-by-step approach ensures that even those with no prior Linux experience can follow along, while the advanced topics provide valuable insights for more experienced users.

For beginners, the book offers a gentle introduction to the Linux environment, gradually building your confidence as you learn to navigate the command line, manage files, and understand the Linux file system hierarchy. IT professionals transitioning from other operating systems will find the comparisons and contrasts between Linux and other platforms particularly helpful. The book's focus on practical, real-world scenarios ensures that you can immediately apply what you learn to your work environment.

Aspiring system administrators will find this book invaluable in their journey towards RHCSA certification. The book covers all the topics required for the exam, providing in-depth explanations and hands-on exercises to reinforce your learning. By the time you finish the book, you'll have the knowledge and skills needed to confidently sit for the RHCSA exam and take your career to the next level.

What will you gain from reading "Mastering Linux: From Zero to RHCSA"? First and foremost, you'll develop a deep understanding of Linux and its underlying principles. This knowledge will serve as a solid foundation for your future growth in the field of system administration. You'll gain practical skills that are immediately applicable in real-world scenarios, from basic system maintenance to advanced troubleshooting techniques.

Moreover, you'll learn how to automate tasks and optimize system performance—skills that are highly valued in today's fast-paced IT environments. The book's focus on security will equip you with the knowledge needed to protect Linux systems from various threats, a critical skill in an era of increasing cyber attacks. You'll also develop problem-solving skills as you work through the various exercises and scenarios presented in the book, honing your ability to think critically and solve complex technical challenges.

Perhaps most importantly, you'll gain the confidence to work with Linux systems in various contexts. Whether you're managing a small network of servers or working with large-scale cloud infrastructure, the skills you learn from this book will be directly applicable. This confidence, combined with the practical knowledge you'll acquire, will open up new career opportunities and position you as a valuable asset in any IT team.

The journey to mastering Linux is not just about memorizing commands or passing an exam. It's about developing a mindset—a way of approaching problems, understanding systems, and continuously learning. Linux, with its vast ecosystem and active community, offers endless opportunities for growth and discovery. As you progress through this book, you'll find yourself not just learning about Linux but becoming part of a global community of developers, administrators, and enthusiasts who are shaping the future of technology.

"Mastering Linux: From Zero to RHCSA" is more than just a guide to passing the RHCSA exam. It's a comprehensive resource that will transform you from a Linux novice to a confident system administrator. By the time you reach the final chapter, you'll have gained not just knowledge but a new perspective on computing and problem-solving. You'll be equipped with the skills to manage complex systems, troubleshoot issues, and contribute to the ever-evolving world of open-source software.

As you embark on this journey, remember that every expert was once a beginner. The world of Linux may seem vast and complex at first, but with each chapter, you'll find yourself growing more comfortable and confident. The skills you'll learn are not just theoretical; they're practical, in-demand abilities that will serve you well throughout your career.

This book is your roadmap to success in the Linux world. It will guide you through the fundamentals, challenge you with advanced concepts, and prepare you for the rigors of professional system administration. Whether your goal is to pass the RHCSA exam, advance your career, or simply gain a deeper understanding of the technology that powers much of our digital world, "Mastering Linux: From Zero to RHCSA" will help you achieve it.

The journey begins with the first command you type, the first system you configure, and the first problem you solve. As you progress through the chapters, you'll find yourself tackling increasingly complex tasks with ease. You'll learn to think like a Linux administrator, approaching challenges with a mix of analytical thinking and creative problem-solving.

One of the most valuable aspects of this book is its focus on hands-on learning. Each chapter includes practical exercises and real-world scenarios that allow you to apply what you've learned immediately. This approach not only reinforces your understanding but also builds muscle memory for common tasks, making you more efficient and effective in your work.

You'll start by setting up your own Linux learning environment, giving you a safe space to experiment and learn without fear of breaking a production system.

As you progress, you'll dive into essential topics like user and group management, where you'll learn how to create and manage user accounts, set up groups, and configure access controls. These skills are fundamental to any Linux system and form the foundation of effective system administration.

The book then takes you deeper into the world of Linux, exploring topics like storage management and file systems. You'll learn how to partition disks, manage logical volumes, and work with different file systems. These skills are crucial for managing data effectively and ensuring optimal system performance.

As you advance, you'll delve into more complex topics like process and service management. You'll learn how to monitor system resources, manage services using systemd, and configure startup and shutdown procedures. These skills are essential for maintaining system stability and ensuring that critical services are always available.

Networking is another crucial area covered in depth. You'll learn how to configure network interfaces, resolve DNS issues, and troubleshoot common networking problems. In today's interconnected world, these skills are indispensable for any system administrator.

Security is a major focus of the book, reflecting its critical importance in today's digital landscape. You'll learn how to implement firewalls, work with SELinux, secure SSH access, and audit system security. These skills will enable you to protect your systems from a wide range of threats and ensure the integrity of your data.

The book also covers essential topics like package management and software installation. You'll learn how to use package managers like YUM and DNF, manage software repositories, and even compile software from source. These skills will allow you to keep your systems up-to-date and install the software needed to meet your organization's needs.

System monitoring and logging are also covered in depth. You'll learn how to configure system logging, analyze log files, monitor system performance, and create cron jobs for automated tasks. These skills are crucial for identifying and resolving issues before they impact system performance or user experience.

Finally, the book covers backup, recovery, and system maintenance. You'll learn how to implement effective backup strategies, restore systems from backups, update and patch systems, and troubleshoot boot issues. These skills are essential for ensuring business continuity and minimizing downtime in the event of system failures.

Throughout the book, you'll find tips and best practices gleaned from real-world experience. These insights will help you avoid common pitfalls and develop good habits that will serve you well throughout your career. You'll also find discussions of the underlying principles behind various Linux features and commands, helping you understand not just how to do things but why they're done that way.

As you near the end of the book, you'll find yourself well-prepared for the RHCSA exam. But more than that, you'll have developed a comprehensive skill set that will serve you well in any Linux environment. You'll be able to confidently manage Red Hat Enterprise Linux systems, troubleshoot complex issues, and contribute effectively to any IT team.

But your journey doesn't end with the last page of this book. Linux is a constantly evolving ecosystem, and one of the most valuable skills you'll develop is the ability to continue learning and adapting. The book will teach you how to find and use resources effectively, participate in the Linux community, and stay up-to-date with the latest developments in the field.

As you close this introduction and prepare to dive into the first chapter, remember that you're not just learning a set of commands or procedures. You're embarking on a journey that will change the way you think about computing. problem-solving, and technology as a whole. You're joining a global community of Linux users and contributors, becoming part of a movement that's shaping the future of technology.

The path ahead may seem challenging at times, but remember that every expert was once a beginner. With persistence, curiosity, and the guidance provided in this book, you'll soon find yourself navigating the Linux landscape with confidence and skill. So take a deep breath, open your mind, and prepare to enter the fascinating world of Linux. Your journey to mastery begins now.

Chapter 1:

Introduction to Linux and the RHCSA Certification

The journey of a thousand miles begins with a single step, and in the world

of Linux, that first step is understanding its rich history and philosophy. Linux, an

open-source operating system, has revolutionized the computing landscape since

its inception in 1991 by Linus Torvalds. Born out of a desire for a free, Unix-like

operating system, Linux has grown from a hobby project to a cornerstone of

modern computing infrastructure.

The philosophy behind Linux is rooted in the principles of open-source

software development. This philosophy emphasizes collaboration, transparency,

and the freedom to modify and distribute software. Richard Stallman, founder of

the Free Software Foundation, laid the groundwork for this movement with his

GNU Project in 1983. The combination of the GNU tools with Torvalds' kernel

created what we now know as Linux.

As Linus Torvalds himself once said, "Software is like sex; it's better when

it's free." This quip encapsulates the spirit of openness and accessibility that has

driven Linux's development and adoption. The collaborative nature of Linux development has led to rapid innovation and improvement, with thousands of developers worldwide contributing to its growth.

Linux's impact on the technology industry cannot be overstated. It powers everything from smartphones to supercomputers, from web servers to smart TVs. Its flexibility and stability have made it the preferred choice for many enterprises and organizations. The ability to customize and optimize Linux for specific needs has led to the creation of numerous distributions, each tailored to different use cases and user preferences.

Among these distributions, Red Hat Enterprise Linux (RHEL) stands out as a leader in the enterprise space. RHEL, developed by Red Hat, Inc., is designed to meet the needs of commercial environments, offering stability, security, and support that businesses require. First released in 2000, RHEL has become synonymous with enterprise-grade Linux, trusted by Fortune 500 companies and government organizations alike.

RHEL's success lies in its ability to provide a robust, scalable platform for mission-critical workloads. It offers features such as live patching, which allows for kernel updates without system reboots, minimizing downtime. RHEL also includes advanced security features, including SELinux (Security-Enhanced Linux), which provides mandatory access control to enhance system security.

One of RHEL's key strengths is its long-term support model. Each major version of RHEL is supported for up to 10 years, providing businesses with the stability and predictability they need for long-term planning. This support includes not just bug fixes and security updates but also hardware enablement and feature backports, ensuring that RHEL systems remain current and compatible with the latest technologies.

Red Hat's commitment to open-source principles is evident in their development model. While RHEL is a commercial product, its source code is freely available, and many of Red Hat's innovations are contributed back to the broader Linux community. This approach has helped to foster a vibrant ecosystem of compatible distributions, such as CentOS and Fedora, which serve as testing grounds for technologies that may eventually make their way into RHEL.

The popularity and widespread adoption of RHEL in enterprise environments have created a high demand for skilled Linux administrators. This demand has given rise to the Red Hat Certified System Administrator (RHCSA) certification, a highly respected credential in the IT industry. The RHCSA certification validates a professional's ability to perform the core system administration skills required in Red Hat Enterprise Linux environments.

The RHCSA certification covers a wide range of essential skills, including system configuration, service management, storage configuration, and security implementation. Candidates are expected to demonstrate proficiency in tasks such as managing users and groups, configuring network interfaces, managing software packages, and troubleshooting system issues. These skills are tested through hands-on, performance-based exams that simulate real-world scenarios, ensuring that certified professionals are truly capable of managing RHEL systems effectively.

Obtaining the RHCSA certification offers numerous benefits for IT professionals. Firstly, it provides clear validation of one's skills, increasing employability and career prospects. Many organizations specifically seek RHCSA-certified professionals for their Linux administration roles. Secondly, the certification process itself serves as an excellent learning experience, pushing candidates to deepen their understanding of Linux systems and best practices.

Moreover, the RHCSA certification serves as a stepping stone to more advanced Red Hat certifications, such as the Red Hat Certified Engineer (RHCE) and Red Hat Certified Architect (RHCA). This clear certification path allows professionals to continually develop their skills and advance their careers in the Linux ecosystem.

As Jim Whitehurst, former CEO of Red Hat, once stated, "The beauty of open source is that it's a self-correcting system. The nature of it is that if there's a flaw, someone will find it and fix it." This principle extends to the learning process as well. The journey to RHCSA certification is not just about passing an exam; it's about becoming part of a community of learners and contributors, constantly improving and adapting to new challenges.

To embark on this journey, setting up a proper learning environment is crucial. While RHEL is a commercial product, there are several ways to gain hands-on experience without incurring significant costs. One option is to take advantage of Red Hat's Developer Subscription, which provides access to RHEL for development purposes at no cost. This allows aspiring administrators to work with the actual operating system they'll be managing in professional environments.

Another popular option is to use CentOS, a free, community-supported distribution that is binary compatible with RHEL. While CentOS Stream has replaced the traditional CentOS as a downstream project of RHEL, it still provides a valuable platform for learning RHEL-compatible systems. Additionally, virtual machines and containerization technologies like Docker can be used to create isolated environments for experimenting with different configurations and scenarios.

Online labs and practice environments are also valuable resources for RHCSA preparation. These platforms provide pre-configured systems that allow learners to practice tasks and scenarios similar to those encountered in the certification exam. Many of these labs offer guided exercises and instant feedback, helping to reinforce learning and identify areas that need improvement.

As we conclude this introduction to Linux and the RHCSA certification, it's important to remember that mastering Linux is a journey, not a destination. The field of system administration is constantly evolving, with new technologies and best practices emerging regularly. The RHCSA certification is just the beginning of a lifelong learning process in the world of Linux.

In the next chapter, we'll dive into the fundamental building blocks of Linux administration: basic commands and file system navigation. These skills form the foundation upon which all higher-level system administration tasks are built. By mastering these basics, you'll be well-prepared to tackle more complex topics as we progress through the book.

Chapter 2:

Basic Linux Commands and File System Navigation

As we delve deeper into the world of Linux, it's crucial to understand the fundamental building blocks that form the basis of interaction with this powerful operating system. In this chapter, we'll explore the command-line interface, the file system hierarchy, essential commands for manipulating files and directories, and the intricacies of file permissions and ownership. These concepts are not only vital for day-to-day operations but also form the foundation for more advanced Linux administration tasks.

The command-line interface (CLI) is the heart of Linux systems, offering unparalleled power and flexibility to users and administrators alike. Unlike graphical user interfaces (GUIs) that are common in consumer-oriented operating systems, the CLI provides direct access to the system's core functions through text-based commands. This interface might seem daunting at first, but its efficiency and versatility become apparent as you gain familiarity.

To begin working with the CLI, you typically open a terminal emulator in your Linux environment. This terminal window acts as your gateway to the command line. The highlighted prompt you see in the quote is usually a combination of your:

- ❖ *username,*
- ❖ *hostname* and
- ❖ *current directory, followed by a symbol like $ or #.*

For example, you might see something like **"user@hostname:~$"**. This prompt is your cue to enter commands. See a real-life example from my Rhel9 server in the figure below:

Figure 1

user@hostname:~$ = obert@server3 ~] $

One of the first commands you should become familiar with is '*pwd*', which stands for **"print working directory."** This command displays your current location within the file system. When you execute '*pwd*', you might see output like *"/home/username"*, indicating that you're in your home directory. Understanding your current location is crucial, as many commands operate relative to this position. See the figure below:

```
[obert@server3 ~]$ pwd
/home/obert
[obert@server3 ~]$ █
```

Moving around the file system is accomplished with the *'cd'* (change directory) command. For instance, *'cd /etc'* would take you to the system configuration directory, while *'cd ~'* would return you to your home directory. The tilde (~) is a shorthand for the current user's home directory in Linux. Mastering directory navigation is essential for efficient system management.

See figure below from my rhel9 server3:

Looking at this terminal, you will notice that before running **cd /etc**, I was at my home directory, represented by the tilde (~) sign. But after running the command, I was completely at a different location in the filesystem, **/etc**, to be precise.

As you navigate the file system, you'll encounter the File System Hierarchy Standard (FHS), a set of guidelines that define the directory structure and directory contents in Linux and other Unix-like operating systems. Understanding this hierarchy is crucial for effective system administration and troubleshooting.

At the root of the file system is the '/' directory, from which all other directories branch out. Some key directories include:

- ❖ *home: Contains user home directories*
- ❖ */etc: Holds system configuration files*
- ❖ */var: Contains variable data like logs and temporary files*
- ❖ */usr: Stores user programs and data*
- ❖ */bin and /sbin: Contain essential system binaries*
- ❖ */tmp: Used for temporary files*

Each of these directories serves a specific purpose, and knowing their roles helps in locating files and understanding system organization. For example, if you're looking for a user's personal files (example, obert), you'd navigate to **/home/username = /home/obert**. If you need to modify system-wide configurations, you'd likely find the relevant files in /etc. The figure below intends to show you how I could view files in my home directory while already there and

how I could still view them from anywhere in the filesystem (for example, from
the /etc directory), respectively.

```
[obert@server3 ~]$ ls
Desktop    Downloads  Pictures  Templates  Videos
Documents  Music      Public    Tutorials
```

```
[obert@server3 etc]$ ls /home/obert/
Desktop    Downloads  Pictures  Templates  Videos
Documents  Music      Public    Tutorials
[obert@server3 etc]$ ls ~
Desktop    Downloads  Pictures  Templates  Videos
Documents  Music      Public    Tutorials
[obert@server3 etc]$
```

As you explore the file system, you'll often need to list directory contents.
The '*ls*' command is your go-to tool for this task. In its simplest form, '*ls*'
displays the contents of the current directory. However, it becomes much more
powerful when combined with various options. For instance, '*ls -l*' provides a
long listing format, showing detailed information about each file, including
permissions, owner, size, and modification date. '*ls -a*' shows all files, including
hidden ones (those starting with a dot), while *-R*' recursively lists subdirectories.
See it below in my server3. Let's see it in practice in the figures below.

ls -R:

```
[root@server3 ~]# ls -R
.:
anaconda-ks.cfg  Desktop  Documents  Downloads  initial-setup-ks.cfg  Music  Pictures  Public  Templates  Videos

./Desktop:
learn1

./Documents:
learn1

./Downloads:
down.txt

./Music:

./Pictures:
pic1

./Public:
pup.txt

./Templates:

./Videos:
clp.mp4
[root@server3 ~]#
```

ls -a:

```
[root@server3 ~]# ls -a
.                          Music
..                         Pictures
anaconda-ks.cfg            .pki
.bash_history              Public
.bash_logout               .tcshrc
.bash_profile              Templates
.bashrc                    .vboxclient-clipboard-tty2-control.pid
.cache                     .vboxclient-clipboard-tty2-service.pid
.config                    .vboxclient-draganddrop-tty2-control.pid
.cshrc                     .vboxclient-draganddrop-tty2-service.pid
.dbus                      .vboxclient-hostversion-tty2-control.pid
Desktop                    .vboxclient-seamless-tty2-control.pid
Documents                  .vboxclient-seamless-tty2-service.pid
Downloads                  .vboxclient-vmsvga-session-tty2-control.pid
.esd_auth                  .vboxclient-vmsvga-session-tty2-service.pid
.ICEauthority              Videos
initial-setup-ks.cfg       .xauthyJO72i
.local
[root@server3 ~]# ls -R
.:
```

ls -l:

```
[root@server3 ~]# ls -l
total 8
-rw-------. 1 root root 1751 Aug  3 11:38 anaconda-ks.cfg
drwxr-xr-x. 2 root root   28 Oct 22 02:02 Desktop
drwxr-xr-x. 2 root root   29 Oct 22 02:02 Documents
drwxr-xr-x. 2 root root   22 Oct 22 02:04 Downloads
-rw-r--r--. 1 root root 2004 Aug  3 11:37 initial-setup-ks.cfg
drwxr-xr-x. 2 root root    6 Oct 22 00:39 Music
drwxr-xr-x. 2 root root   16 Oct 22 02:03 Pictures
drwxr-xr-x. 2 root root   21 Oct 22 02:03 Public
drwxr-xr-x. 2 root root    6 Oct 22 00:39 Templates
drwxr-xr-x. 2 root root   21 Oct 22 02:05 Videos
[root@server3 ~]#
[root@server3 ~]#
```

File manipulation is a cornerstone of Linux administration, and several commands are essential for these operations. The '*cp*' command copies files and directories. For example, 'cp file1 file2' creates a copy of file1 named file2. To copy entire directories and their contents, you'd use 'cp -r dir1 dir2'. Let's look at these real-life examples below:

Copying file1 to another file called file2:

```
[obert@server3 ~]$ ls
Desktop  Documents  Downloads  file1  file3  learning{1  learning.txt{1  Music  Pictures  Public  Templates  Tutorials  Videos
[obert@server3 ~]$ cp file1 file2
[obert@server3 ~]$ ls
Desktop  Documents  Downloads  file1  file2  file3  learning{1  learning.txt{1  Music  Pictures  Public  Templates  Tutorials  Videos
[obert@server3 ~]$ cat file1 file2
This is a copy (cp) test
This is a copy (cp) test
[obert@server3 ~]$
```

The 'mv' command is used both for moving files and renaming them. 'mv oldname newname' renames a file, while 'mv file /path/to/destination/' moves the file to a new location. Let's move (rename) file1 to file4 and move file2 (relocate) to a new location/directory called cuments, respectively.

Renaming file1 to file4:

```
[obert@server3 ~]$ ls
Desktop  Documents  Downloads  file1  file2  file3  learning{1  learning.txt{1  Music  Pictures  Public  Templates  Tutorials  Videos
[obert@server3 ~]$ mv file1 file4
[obert@server3 ~]$ ls
Desktop  Documents  Downloads  file2  file3  file4  learning{1  learning.txt{1  Music  Pictures  Public  Templates  Tutorials  Videos
[obert@server3 ~]$ cat file4
This is a copy (cp) test
I have just been moved
[obert@server3 ~]$
```

30

Moving file4 to a new location:

```
[obert@server3 ~]$ ls
Desktop  Documents  Downloads  file3  file4  learning{1  learning.txt{1  Music  Pictures  Public  Templates  Tutorials  Videos
[obert@server3 ~]$ ls Documents/cuments/doc/
[obert@server3 ~]$ cat file4
This is a copy (cp) test
I have just been moved
[obert@server3 ~]$ mv file4 Documents/cuments/doc/
[obert@server3 ~]$ ls Documents/cuments/doc/
file4
[obert@server3 ~]$ ls
Desktop  Documents  Downloads  file3  learning{1  learning.txt{1  Music  Pictures  Public  Templates  Tutorials  Videos
[obert@server3 ~]$ ▮
```

Creating new directories is done with the '**mkdir**' command. '**mkdir**

newdir' creates a directory named "newdir" in the current location. For creating

nested directories, the ' *-p*' option is useful: *'mkdir -p*

parent/child/grandchild' creates the entire directory structure in one

command. Let us do that too.

Creating the newdir directory in the current directory:

```
[obert@server3 ~]$ ls
Desktop  Documents  Downloads  file3  learning{1  learning.txt{1  Music  Pictures  Public  Templates  Tutorials  Videos
[obert@server3 ~]$ mkdir newdir
[obert@server3 ~]$ ls
Desktop  Documents  Downloads  file3  learning{1  learning.txt{1  Music  newdir  Pictures  Public  Templates  Tutorials  Videos
```

Creating the nested directory called austin:

```
[obert@server3 ~]$ mkdir -p usa/texas/austin
[obert@server3 ~]$ ls
Desktop  Documents  Downloads  file3  learning{1  learning.txt{1  Music  newdir  Pictures  Public  Templates  Tutorials  usa  Videos
[obert@server3 ~]$ ls usa/texas
austin
[obert@server3 ~]$ ▮
```

31

You see how the austin directory is created in the format of parent/child/grandchild where:

usa/ = parent

texas/ = child

austin/ = grandchild

Removing files and directories requires caution, as these operations are often irreversible. The '**rm**' command deletes files, while '**rmdir**' removes empty directories. To delete a directory and all its contents, you'd use '**rm** **-r** directory'. It's crucial to double-check your commands when using '**rm**', especially with sudo privileges, as accidental deletions can have severe consequences. Let's see this done in the examples below:

Deleting files: we shall delete file3 and the newdir directory, respectively.

I verified each action taken, and the expected results were attained.

Text manipulation is another crucial skill in Linux administration. The '*cat*' command is used to display file contents, while '**less**' allows for scrollable viewing of larger files. For searching within files, '*grep*' is an indispensable tool. For example, '*grep* "**error**" logfile.txt/anyfile' would display all lines containing the word "error" in logfile.txt. But we could search whatever using the grep command; we just have to know where to search. Below I have shared a few locations of common Log files in Rhel8, and we will explore a couple of them for practice.

Log Files	Location	Description
Systems Log	/var/log/messages	General system log, including boot information, errors, etc.
Kernel	/var/log/kern.log	Kenel-related messages. Might be combined in /var/log/messages.
Authentication Log	/var/log/secure	Authentication-related events (login attempts, sudo, etc)
Boot Log	/var/log/boot.log	Boot-up process and service startup information.
Cron Logs	/var/log/cron	Logs related to cron jobs and scheduled tasks.
Systemd Journal	Journalctl command	Logs managed by systemd. Can be accessed through journalctl

Xorg Log	/var/log/Xorg.0.log	Logs for X11 server if running a graphical environment

Let us concatenate (cat) a file called zero2rhcsa in my rhel8 and grep the Authentication Log, respectively. Please refer to the table above for the location of the authentication log if you are following along.

```
[obert@server3 ~]$ ls
Desktop    Downloads    learning.txt[1  Pictures  Templates  usa      zero2rhcsa
Documents  learning[1   Music         Public    Tutorials  Videos
[obert@server3 ~]$ cat zero2rhcsa
200-Ansible Core Documentation

Ansible Core, or ansible-core is the main building block and architecture for Ansible, and includes:

    CLI tools such as ansible-playbook, ansible-doc, and others for driving and interacting with automati
on.

    The Ansible language that uses YAML to create a set of rules for developing Ansible Playbooks and inc
ludes functions such as conditionals, blocks, includes, loops, and other Ansible imperatives.

    An architectural framework that allows extensions through Ansible collections.

This documentation covers the version of ansible-core noted in the upper left corner of this page. We mai
ntain multiple versions of ansible-core and of the documentation, so please be sure you are using the ver
sion of the documentation that covers the version of Ansible you're using. For recent features, we note t
he version of Ansible where the feature was added.

ansible-core releases a new major release approximately twice a year. The core application evolves somewh
at conservatively, valuing simplicity in language design and setup. Contributors develop and change modul
es and plugins, hosted in collections, much more quickly.
Introduction to Ansible
```

Let us grep something particular within the Authentication Log file (secure) and experience how it works first-hand. Let us search for 'rules' in the Authentication Log file.

```
[obert@server3 log]$ sudo grep rules secure
Oct 16 10:15:20 server3 polkitd[952]: Error evaluating authorization rules
Oct 16 17:16:57 server3 polkitd[952]: Error evaluating authorization rules
Oct 16 17:17:07 server3 polkitd[952]: Error evaluating authorization rules
Oct 16 17:17:18 server3 polkitd[952]: Error evaluating authorization rules
Oct 18 23:01:40 server3 polkitd[952]: Error evaluating authorization rules
Oct 21 16:52:41 server3 polkitd[938]: Loading rules from directory /etc/polkit-1/rules.d
Oct 21 16:52:41 server3 polkitd[938]: Loading rules from directory /usr/share/polkit-1/rules.d
Oct 21 16:52:41 server3 polkitd[938]: Finished loading, compiling and executing 12 rules
Oct 21 19:06:48 server3 polkitd[938]: Loading rules from directory /etc/polkit-1/rules.d
Oct 21 19:06:48 server3 polkitd[938]: Loading rules from directory /usr/share/polkit-1/rules.d
Oct 21 19:06:48 server3 polkitd[938]: Finished loading, compiling and executing 12 rules
Oct 21 23:55:28 server3 polkitd[948]: Loading rules from directory /etc/polkit-1/rules.d
Oct 21 23:55:28 server3 polkitd[948]: Loading rules from directory /usr/share/polkit-1/rules.d
Oct 21 23:55:28 server3 polkitd[948]: Finished loading, compiling and executing 12 rules
Oct 21 23:56:59 server3 polkitd[948]: Error evaluating authorization rules
Oct 22 00:04:33 server3 polkitd[948]: Error evaluating authorization rules
Oct 22 00:38:52 server3 polkitd[948]: Error evaluating authorization rules
Oct 22 00:39:14 server3 polkitd[948]: Error evaluating authorization rules
Oct 22 00:42:21 server3 polkitd[959]: Loading rules from directory /etc/polkit-1/rules.d
Oct 22 00:42:21 server3 polkitd[959]: Loading rules from directory /usr/share/polkit-1/rules.d
Oct 22 00:42:21 server3 polkitd[959]: Finished loading, compiling and executing 12 rules
Oct 22 00:43:37 server3 polkitd[959]: Error evaluating authorization rules
Oct 22 00:43:48 server3 polkitd[959]: Error evaluating authorization rules
Oct 22 05:05:01 server3 polkitd[959]: Error evaluating authorization rules
Oct 22 16:00:13 server3 polkitd[955]: Loading rules from directory /etc/polkit-1/rules.d
Oct 22 16:08:13 server3 polkitd[955]: Loading rules from directory /usr/share/polkit-1/rules.d
Oct 22 16:08:13 server3 polkitd[955]: Finished loading, compiling and executing 12 rules
Oct 22 16:09:40 server3 polkitd[955]: Error evaluating authorization rules
Oct 22 16:09:53 server3 polkitd[955]: Error evaluating authorization rules
Oct 22 16:12:28 server3 polkitd[955]: Error evaluating authorization rules
Oct 23 00:13:51 server3 sudo[142417]:    obert : TTY=pts/0 ; PWD=/var/log ; USER=root ; COMMAND=/bin/grep warning rules
[obert@server3 log]$ 
```

File editing is often done using text editors like 'nano' or 'vim'. While 'nano' is more user-friendly for beginners, 'vim' offers powerful features for advanced users. Learning at least one text editor is crucial for tasks like modifying configuration files or writing scripts.

As you work with files and directories, understanding file permissions and ownership becomes crucial. In Linux, every file and directory has associated permissions that determine who can read, write, or execute them. These permissions are divided into three categories displaying the structure of the file permissions:

❖ Owner/user (u): The owner of the file.

❖ Group (g): The group to which the file belongs.

❖ Others (o): All other users.

The 'ls -l' command reveals these permissions in a format like *"rwxr-xr-x."* Here, the first three characters represent the owner's permissions, the next three the group's permissions, and the last three the permissions for others.

❖ 'r' (4) stands for read.

❖ 'w' (2) for write.

❖ 'x' (1) for execute (or access, in the case of directories).

Example in the figure below where I listed my home directory. The reason you see those files belonging to another group is that I forgot not to update all files owned by the former mrsho user to user obert.

Looking at those files, you see the permission signs we talked about above. Worry not about the letter 'd' in front of them. We will discuss that later.

Modifying permissions is done with the 'chmod' command. For instance, 'chmod 755 fileName' sets read(4), write(2), and execute(1) permissions for the owner, and read and execute permissions for groups and others. The numeric representation (755 in this case) is a shorthand where each digit represents the permissions for owner, group, and others, respectively, with 4 for read, 2 for write, and 1 for execute. Adding these numbers, for example:

* ❖ *rwx = 4+2+1 = 7 owner*
* ❖ *r-x = 4+1 = 5   group*
* ❖ *r-x = 4+1 = 5   other*

Looking at the screenshot below, you will see a file called file1, owned by the root user, and it belongs in the root group. The owner (root), group and others do not have the execute permission. Let's give the execute permission of this file to the owner, using the chmod command; he deserves it.

```
[root@server3 ~]# ls -l
total 12
-rw-------. 1 root root 1751 Aug  3 11:38 anaconda-ks.cfg
drwxr-xr-x. 2 root root   20 Oct 22 02:02 Desktop
drwxr-xr-x. 2 root root   20 Oct 22 02:02 Documents
drwxr-xr-x. 2 root root   22 Oct 22 02:04 Downloads
-rw-r--r--. 1 root root   26 Oct 22 02:25 file1
-rw-r--r--. 1 root root 2084 Aug  3 11:37 initial-setup-ks.cfg
drwxr-xr-x. 2 root root    6 Oct 22 00:39 Music
drwxr-xr-x. 2 root root   18 Oct 22 02:03 Pictures
drwxr-xr-x. 2 root root   21 Oct 22 02:03 Public
drwxr-xr-x. 2 root root    6 Oct 22 00:39 Templates
drwxr-xr-x. 2 root root   21 Oct 22 02:05 Videos
[root@server3 ~]#
```

The new screenshot below shows the highlighted file1 with execute

permission to the root/owner of the file.

```
[root@server3 ~]# chmod u+x file1
[root@server3 ~]# ls -l
total 12
-rw-------. 1 root root 1751 Aug  3 11:38 anaconda-ks.cfg
drwxr-xr-x. 2 root root   20 Oct 22 02:02 Desktop
drwxr-xr-x. 2 root root   20 Oct 22 02:02 Documents
drwxr-xr-x. 2 root root   22 Oct 22 02:04 Downloads
-rwxr-xr--. 1 root root   26 Oct 22 02:25 file1
-rw-r--r--. 1 root root 2084 Aug  3 11:37 initial-setup-ks.cfg
drwxr-xr-x. 2 root root    6 Oct 22 00:39 Music
drwxr-xr-x. 2 root root   18 Oct 22 02:03 Pictures
drwxr-xr-x. 2 root root   21 Oct 22 02:03 Public
drwxr-xr-x. 2 root root    6 Oct 22 00:39 Templates
drwxr-xr-x. 2 root root   21 Oct 22 02:05 Videos
[root@server3 ~]#
```

Ownership of files and directories is another critical aspect of Linux security.

The '*chown*' command changes the owner of a file, while '*chgrp*' changes the group

ownership of a file and a directory. For example, *'chown user:group* file' changes

both the owner and group of the file in one command. But what if you want to
change only the group ownership? The *chgrp* changes group ownership of a file or
directory, which is very useful when an admin wants to assign a file or directory to
a different group. Let us practice this by changing file1 owner and group to user
obert. Then we shall change the group ownership of zero2rhcsa file from obert to
root.

```
[root@server3 ~]# chown obert:obert file1
[root@server3 ~]# ls
anaconda-ks.cfg  Documents  file1                Music      Public     Videos
Desktop          Downloads  initial-setup-ks.cfg Pictures   Templates
[root@server3 ~]# ls -l
total 12
-rw-------. 1 root   root   1751 Aug  3 11:38 anaconda-ks.cfg
drwxr-xr-x. 2 root   root     20 Oct 22 02:02 Desktop
drwxr-xr-x. 2 root   root     20 Oct 22 02:02 Documents
drwxr-xr-x. 2 root   root     22 Oct 22 02:04 Downloads
-rwxr--r--. 1 obert  obert    26 Oct 22 02:25 file1
-rw-r--r--. 1 root   root   2084 Aug  3 11:37 initial-setup-ks.cfg
drwxr-xr-x. 2 root   root      6 Oct 22 00:39 Music
drwxr-xr-x. 2 root   root     18 Oct 22 02:03 Pictures
drwxr-xr-x. 2 root   root     21 Oct 22 02:03 Public
drwxr-xr-x. 2 root   root      6 Oct 22 00:39 Templates
drwxr-xr-x. 2 root   root     21 Oct 22 02:05 Videos
[root@server3 ~]#
```

Understanding these basic commands and concepts is fundamental to becoming proficient in Linux administration. They form the building blocks for more advanced operations and are used daily by system administrators and power users alike. As you progress through your Linux journey, you'll find yourself combining these commands in increasingly complex ways to achieve specific tasks efficiently.

As we conclude this chapter on basic Linux commands and file system navigation, it's important to remember that practice is key to mastering these concepts. Regular use of these commands will help solidify your understanding and improve your efficiency in working with Linux systems. In the next chapter, we'll build upon this foundation as we explore user and group management,

delving deeper into the security and administrative aspects of Linux systems.

Chapter 3:

User and Group Management

As we delve deeper into the intricacies of Linux system administration, it becomes crucial to understand the fundamental concepts of user and group management. Building upon the basic commands and file system navigation we explored in the previous chapter, we now turn our attention to the critical task of managing user accounts and groups within a Linux environment. This chapter will equip you with the knowledge and skills necessary to create and manage user accounts, administer groups, implement robust password policies, and configure *sudo* access for privileged operations. Before we do, here are a few examples of how to navigate the Linux filesystem. The *cd* command is used in Linux, Unix, and Windows systems to change the current working directory within the command line interface (CLI). For example, within my home directory, I can change to the Document directory simply by the following command: *cd Documents/.* We begin by viewing the content of our home directory with *ls* command, then navigate to the Documents directory. Look at the highlighted. You noticed how the tilde sign denoting I am in my home directory immediately changed to the Documents/

directory. This means I have moved down away from the parent directory. A *cd ~* will move me back to the parent directory.

```
                              obert@server3:~                              ×
 File  Edit  View  Search  Terminal  Help
[obert@server3 ~]$ ls
ansible quickstart  Documents    learning.txt{1  Public     usa
Desktop             Downloads    Music           Templates  Videos
dhcp.txt            learning{1   Pictures        Tutorials  zero2rhcsa
[obert@server3 ~]$ cd Documents/
[obert@server3 Documents]$ ls
cuments
[obert@server3 Documents]$ cd ~
[obert@server3 ~]$ █
```

User accounts form the cornerstone of any multi-user operating system, and Linux is no exception. In fact, the ability to support multiple users simultaneously is one of the key strengths of Linux, allowing for efficient resource sharing and collaboration while maintaining security and privacy. Each user account in Linux is associated with a unique identifier, known as the *User ID (UID),* which the system uses to track and manage user-specific information and permissions. We should have a look into the UID of user *obert* on this rhel8. To achieve that, we use just the *id*, or the id command and the *username* depending on who want to view the information, like this '*id obert'.* The example shows myself viewing my UID and another root viewing it.

```
[obert@server3 ~]$ id
uid=1000(obert) gid=1000(obert) groups=1000(obert),10(wheel) context=unconfined_
u:unconfined_r:unconfined_t:s0-s0:c0.c1023
[obert@server3 ~]$ su -
Password:
[root@server3 ~]# id obert
uid=1000(obert) gid=1000(obert) groups=1000(obert),10(wheel)
```

Let's begin by exploring the process of creating and managing user accounts. The primary command for this purpose is '*useradd*', which allows system administrators to add new users to the system. For example, to create a new user account named 'reader', you would use the following command:

sudo useradd reader

Before we begin, lets list all the users on this rhel8 I am working on so we can experience when a new user is added. We shall use the following command to accomplish this: ***cut -d: -f1 /etc/passwd***. The output of the command includes regular and system users.

```
[root@server3 etc]# cut -d: -f1 /etc/passwd
root
bin
daemon
adm
lp
sync
shutdown
halt
mail
operator
games
ftp
nobody
dbus
systemd-coredump
systemd-resolve
tss
polkitd
unbound
gluster
geoclue
rtkit
pipewire
pulse
qemu
apache
cockpit-ws
cockpit-wsinstance
clevis
named
usbmuxd
postfix
rpc
chrony
avahi
setroubleshoot
saslauth
libstoragemgmt
dnsmasq
sssd
pegasus
flatpak
pcp
colord
rpcuser
gdm
abrt
```

```
abrt
gnome-initial-setup
pesign
sshd
dovecot
dovenull
tcpdump
grafana
vboxadd
obert
[root@server3 etc]#
```

Now let's create our new user 'reader' without specifying a home directory,

verify, then modify the default.

```
                              obert@server3:~                              ×
File   Edit   View   Search   Terminal   Help
[obert@server3 ~]$ sudo useradd reader
[obert@server3 ~]$ grep '^reader:' /etc/passwd
reader:x:1001:1001::/home/reader:/bin/bash
[obert@server3 ~]$ echo $HOME reader
/home/obert reader
[obert@server3 ~]$
```

Upon creation, a home directory is implicitly created despite not specifying

a home directory be created. This was possible because certain configuration files

were already on this rhel8 modified. The specific file that was modified is

/etc/login.defs, and the CREATE_HOME was set to yes:

```
# If useradd should create home directories for users by default
# On RH systems, we do. This option is overridden with the -m flag on
# useradd command line.
#
CREATE_HOME     yes
```

Without modification to the file, this command creates a new user account with default settings. However, in most cases, you'll want to customize various aspects of the account creation process. For instance, you might want to specify a home directory, set an initial password, or define the user's default shell. The 'useradd' command provides numerous options to achieve this level of customization.

One common practice is to create a home directory for the new user at the time of account creation. This can be done using the '-m' option:

sudo useradd -m reader

This command not only creates the user account but also sets up a home directory at '/home/reader'. The system populates this directory with default configuration files, ensuring that the new user has a functional environment from the moment they first log in. I made some changes to the */etc/login.defs* file, setting the CREAT_HOME = no, so that we can experience the difference. I have created a user called "readrr" using the *useradd* readrr command. This user will not have a home directory. To prove that, we shall attempt to change the directory to its home directory and see what happens; it should fail. To confirm that, we shall do the

same to user Obert who was created using option -m or before modifying the file.

```
[root@server3 ~]# cd /home/readrr
-bash: cd: /home/readrr: No such file or directory
[root@server3 ~]#
[root@server3 ~]#
```

```
[root@server3 reading]# cd /home/obert/
[root@server3 obert]# ls
ansible quickstart  Documents   learning.txt{1  Public     usa
Desktop             Downloads   Music           Templates  Videos
dhcp.txt            learning{1  Pictures        Tutorials  zero2rhcsa
```

Once a user account is created, you may need to modify its properties. The

'usermod' command comes in handy for this purpose. For example, to change the

home directory of an existing user, you would use:

  sudo usermod -d /newhome/reader reader. This command changes the

home directory of the user 'reader' to *'/newhome/reader'*.

```
[root@server3 ~]#
[root@server3 ~]# mkdir /rhcsa
[root@server3 ~]# usermod -d /rhcsa/reader reader
```

```
[root@server3 reader]# grep '^reader:' /etc/passwd
reader:x:1001:1001::/rhcsa/reader:/bin/bash
```

It's important to note that this command only changes the entry in the system's user database; it doesn't actually move the user's files. To physically move the contents of the old home directory to the new location, you would need to use the *'mv'* command separately.

sudo mv /home/reader/* /rhcsa/reader .... Moving files

sudo mv /home/reader/.* /rhcsa/reader .... Moving hiding files, and verify the changes done so far : *grep '^reader:' /etc/passwd*

As systems evolve and organizational needs change, there may come a time when you need to remove user accounts. The *'userdel'* command is used for this purpose. By default, this command only removes the user's entry from the system's user database, leaving their home directory and mail spool intact. To remove the user's home directory and mail spool along with the account, you would use the *'-r'* option:

sudo userdel -r readers

It's crucial to exercise caution when using this command, as it permanently deletes the user's data. Always ensure that any important data has been backed up before proceeding with account deletion. Let's delete user *readers* with all data and verify deletion status.

```
readers:x:1002:1002::/home/readers:/bin/bash
reading:x:1003:1003::/home/reading:/bin/bash
readrr:x:1004:1004::/home/readrr:/bin/bash
[obert@server3 ~]$
[obert@server3 ~]$
[obert@server3 ~]$ grep '^reader:' /etc/passwd
[obert@server3 ~]$ sudo userdel -r readers
[sudo] password for obert:
[obert@server3 ~]$
[obert@server3 ~]$ grep '^readers:' /etc/passwd
[obert@server3 ~]$ grep '^obert:' /etc/passwd
obert:x:1000:1000:MRSHO:/home/obert:/bin/bash
[obert@server3 ~]$
```

Moving on to group management, we find that groups in Linux serve as a powerful mechanism for organizing users and controlling access to system resources. Each user in Linux belongs to at least one group, known as their primary group, and can be a member of multiple secondary groups. Groups are identified by their Group ID (GID), similar to how users are identified by their UID.

The primary command for creating new groups is *'groupadd'*. For instance, to create a new group named 'developers', you would use:

sudo groupadd developers

Once a group is created, you can add users to it using the *'usermod'* command with the *'-aG'* option. For example, to add the user *'obert'* to the 'developers' group:

sudo usermod -aG developers obert

This command adds **'obert'** to the 'developers' group without removing them from any other groups they might belong to. The **'-a'** option is crucial here, as it tells the system to add the user to the specified group without removing them from their current groups. Let's create the developers group on this rhel8 and add user **obert.**

```
File  Edit  View  Search  Terminal  Help
[obert@server3 ~]$ groupadd developers
groupadd: Permission denied.
groupadd: cannot lock /etc/group; try again later.
[obert@server3 ~]$ sudo groupadd developers
[sudo] password for obert:
[obert@server3 ~]$ cat /etc/group |grep developers
developers:x:1005:
[obert@server3 ~]$ sudo usermod -aG developers o
obert        operator
[obert@server3 ~]$ sudo usermod -aG developers o
obert        operator
[obert@server3 ~]$ groups obert
obert : obert wheel
[obert@server3 ~]$ sudo usermod -aG developers obert
[sudo] password for obert:
[obert@server3 ~]$ groups obert
obert : obert wheel developers
[obert@server3 ~]$ 
```

To remove a user from a group, you can use the 'gpasswd' command with the '-d' option:

> **sudo gpasswd -d obert developers ... remove user.**

> **sudo gpasswd -a obert developers ... add user.**

This command removes **'obert'** from the 'developers' group. Let's experience that.

```
[obert@server3 ~]$ groups obert
obert : obert wheel developers
[obert@server3 ~]$ sudo gpasswd -d obert developers
[sudo] password for obert:
Removing user obert from group developers
[obert@server3 ~]$ groups obert
obert : obert wheel
[obert@server3 ~]$ ▮
```

As we progress in our understanding of user and group management, it's important to recognize the significance of password policies in maintaining system security. Linux provides robust mechanisms for enforcing password complexity and aging rules, helping to protect against unauthorized access.

The '*chage*' command is a powerful tool for managing password aging policies. For example, to set the maximum number of days a password remains valid for a user:

sudo chage -M 90 obert

This command sets the maximum password age for '*obert'* to 90 days, after which they will be required to change their password.

Additionally, you can use the '*/etc/login.defs*' file to set system-wide password policies. This file contains various directives that control password aging, length requirements, and other security-related settings. For instance, to set a minimum password length of 12 characters for all users, you would add or modify the following line in '*/etc/login.defs*':

PASS_MIN_LEN 12

We shall visit the */etc/login.defs* file, capture the current settings, verify the current password age for user obert, then modify/change user *obert'*s password age to 68 days, the number of days for before 2024 ends.

We shall use *sudo chage -l username* command to check obert's password age:

```
File  Edit  View  Search  Terminal  Help
[obert@server3 ~]$ sudo chage -l obert
[sudo] password for obert:
Sorry, try again.
[sudo] password for obert:
Last password change                                    : never
Password expires                                        : never
Password inactive                                       : never
Account expires                                         : never
Minimum number of days between password change          : 0
Maximum number of days between password change          : 99999
Number of days of warning before password expires       : 7
[obert@server3 ~]$
```

The information displayed reveals user Obert's password settings is not managed. But we can do that right. I will set it such that I must set a new password the next time I login in 2025.

It's worth noting that while these system-wide settings provide a good baseline, they can be overridden on a per-user basis using commands like '*chage*' or by modifying user-specific configuration files. Below is the current setup of the

/etc/login.def files on password controls. Just underneath will be a capture of user

obert's managed password setup.

```
# Password aging controls:
#
#       PASS_MAX_DAYS   Maximum number of days a password may be used.
#       PASS_MIN_DAYS   Minimum number of days allowed between password changes.
#       PASS_MIN_LEN    Minimum acceptable password length.
#       PASS_WARN_AGE   Number of days warning given before a password expires.
#
PASS_MAX_DAYS   99999
PASS_MIN_DAYS   0
PASS_MIN_LEN    5
PASS_WARN_AGE   7
```

```
[obert@server3 ~]$ sudo chage -l obert
sudo: Account or password is expired, reset your password and try again
Current password:
New password:
Retype new password:
Last password change                                    : Oct 24, 2024
Password expires                                        : Dec 31, 2024
Password inactive                                       : never
Account expires                                         : never
Minimum number of days between password change          : 0
Maximum number of days between password change          : 68
Number of days of warning before password expires       : 7
[obert@server3 ~]$
```

Another crucial aspect of user management in Linux is the configuration of

sudo access. The *sudo* (Superuser Do) command allows regular users to execute

specific commands with elevated privileges, providing a more secure alternative to

logging in as the root user.

The primary configuration file for *sudo* is *'/etc/sudoers'*. This file specifies which users or groups are allowed to use *sudo* and what commands they're permitted to execute. While you can edit this file directly using the *'visudo'* command, it's often safer and more convenient to create separate configuration files in the *'/etc/sudoers.d/'* directory.

For example, to give the user *'obert'* permission to run all commands with *sudo,* you could create a file named *'/etc/sudoers.d/obert'* with the following content:

obert ALL=(ALL) ALL

```
[root@server3 ~]# vim /etc/sudoers.d/obert
[root@server3 ~]# ls /etc/sudoers.d/
obert
[root@server3 ~]# cat /etc/sudoers.d/obert
##############
# Given obert absolute power

obert ALL=(ALL) ALL
[root@server3 ~]#
```

```
                              root@server3:~                              x
File  Edit  View  Search  Terminal  Help
##############
# Given obert absolute power

obert ALL=(ALL) ALL
```

This line grants 'obert' the ability to execute any command on any host as any user. However, in practice, it's usually better to limit sudo access to only the specific commands a user needs. For instance, if 'obert' only needs to be able to restart the Apache web server, you might use:

obert ALL=(ALL) /usr/sbin/service apache2 restart

This more restrictive configuration enhances security by limiting the potential damage that could be done if 'oberts' account were to be compromised.

As we conclude our exploration of user and group management, it's important to emphasize the critical role these concepts play in maintaining a secure and well-organized Linux system. Effective user and group management not only facilitates collaboration and resource sharing but also forms the foundation for implementing more advanced security measures.

In the next chapter, we'll build upon these concepts as we delve into storage management and file systems. We'll explore how to partition and format disks, manage logical volumes, create and mount file systems, and implement disk quotas. These skills will further enhance your ability to efficiently manage and secure Linux systems, bringing you one step closer to mastering Linux and achieving your RHCSA certification.

Chapter 4:

Storage Management and File Systems

As we transition from user and group management, we now turn our
attention to the critical aspect of storage management and file systems in Linux.
This chapter builds upon the foundational knowledge established in earlier
sections, delving into the intricacies of how data is organized, stored, and accessed
within a Linux environment. Understanding these concepts is crucial for any Linux
administrator, as efficient storage management directly impacts system
performance, data integrity, and the overall user experience.

Partitioning and formatting disks form the cornerstone of storage
management in Linux. When a new storage device is connected to a Linux system,
it must be properly partitioned and formatted before it can be utilized effectively.
Partitioning allows for the logical division of a physical storage device into
separate sections, each of which can be treated as an independent unit. This process
is essential for organizing data, implementing different file systems, and enhancing
system security by isolating various components of the operating system.

To begin the partitioning process, Linux administrators typically use tools such as *fdisk, gdisk,* or **parted**. These utilities provide a command-line interface for creating, modifying, and deleting partitions on storage devices. For instance, the *fdisk* command is commonly used for partitioning drives with the Master Boot Record (MBR) partitioning scheme, while **gdisk** is preferred for drives using the GUID Partition Table (GPT) scheme, which is more suitable for modern, large-capacity drives.

Let us consider the following example of using *fdisk* to create a new partition on a drive:

 # fdisk /dev/sdb

But we need to know the information about all available or mounted block devices on the Linux machine we are to perform partitioning on. To do this, we use the following command:

 # lsblk

```
[obert@zero2rhcsa ~]$ lsblk
NAME                MAJ:MIN RM   SIZE RO TYPE MOUNTPOINTS
sda                     8:0   0   100G  0 disk
├─sda1                  8:1   0    2M  0 part
├─sda2                  8:2   0    3G  0 part /boot
└─sda3                  8:3   0 78.6G  0 part
  ├─rhel_vbox-root    253:0   0   25G  0 lvm  /
  ├─rhel_vbox-swap    253:1   0 18.6G  0 lvm  [SWAP]
  ├─rhel_vbox-var     253:2   0   15G  0 lvm  /var
  └─rhel_vbox-home    253:3   0   20G  0 lvm  /home
sr0                    11:0   1 1024M  0 rom
```

Upon checking my system, we see in the above picture the primary physical hard disk of 100GB with three primary partitions:

sda: The primary physical hard disk of 100GB

sda1: 2M possibly for BIOS boot

sda2: 3GB mounted on /boot

sda3: 78.6GB, which is a logical volume manager (LVM) partition.

I do not want us to mess with it. We shall mount a second hard disk to be used for the portioning exercise that will automatically be called *sdb*.

Adding a second virtual hard disk requires the following steps be followed:

1 – Open Oracle VirtualBox, select the VM, then click Settings:

2 – Click Storage:

3 – Click the disk symbol with a plus (+) sign and select Hard Disk:

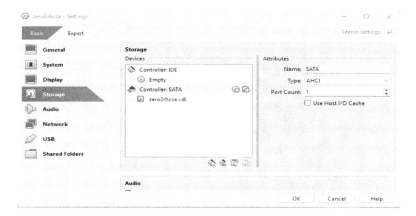

4 – Select CREATE, VIRTUAL HARD DISK, then NEXT:

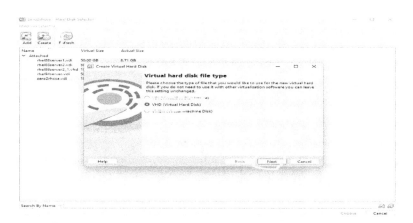

You should click NEXT on the NEXT screen too.

5 – Enter or select the size in GB: I entered 20GB, then click FINISH

rtual Size   Actual Size

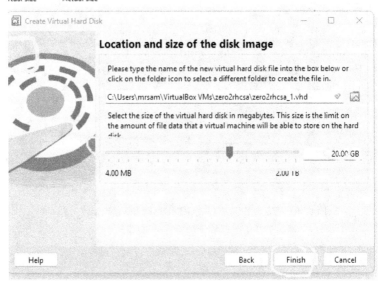

Create Virtual Hard Disk   — ☐ ✕

Location and size of the disk image

Please type the name of the new virtual hard disk file into the box below or
click on the folder icon to select a different folder to create the file in.

C:\Users\mrsam\VirtualBox VMs\zero2rhcsa\zero2rhcsa_1.vhd   ⬦ 🖾

Select the size of the virtual hard disk in megabytes. This size is the limit on
the amount of file data that a virtual machine will be able to store on the hard
disk.

                                                                    20.00 GB

4.00 MB   2.00 TB

Help   Back   Finish   Cancel

6 – Select the HARD DISK you just created and click CHOOSE:

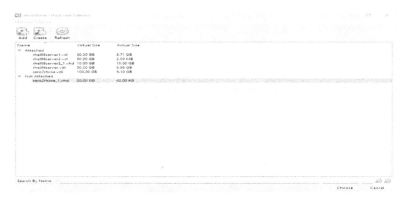

Once you click choose, the current screen will disappear. Make sure to click OK on the next screen in front of you. You are done. Turn on your VM again; you will see a new hard disk *sdb* when you run *lsblk*.

Once *fdisk /dev/sdb* command is executed, we shall follow the prompt, choosing the following options below:

Command (m for help): n... *where n equals the new partition.*

Partition type: p, *where p equals primary partition.*

Partition number: 1... *where 1 equals primary partition.*

First sector: (default) *hit enter to accept the default.*

Last sector: +5G, *where 5G is the partition size.*

Command (m for help): w... *where w is writing in memory changes*

Let's begin partitioning the new virtual hard disk we just created on our

zero2rhcsa vm using the command above:

```
obert@zero2rhcsa:~

[obert@zero2rhcsa ~]$ sudo fdisk /dev/sdb
[sudo] password for obert:
Sorry, try again.
[sudo] password for obert:

Welcome to fdisk (util-linux 2.37.4).
Changes will remain in memory only, until you decide to write them.
Be careful before using the write command.

Device does not contain a recognized partition table.
Created a new DOS disklabel with disk identifier 0x6c55545e.

Command (m for help): n
Partition type
   p   primary (0 primary, 0 extended, 4 free)
   e   extended (container for logical partitions)
Select (default p): p
Partition number (1-4, default 1): 1
First sector (2048-41943039, default 2048):
Last sector, +/-sectors or +/-size{K,M,G,T,P} (2048-41943039, default 41943039):
 +1GB

Created a new partition 1 of type 'Linux' and of size 954 MiB.

Command (m for help): w
The partition table has been altered.
Calling ioctl() to re-read partition table.
Syncing disks.
```

This sequence of commands creates a new primary partition of 1GB on the */dev/sdb* drive. The '*w*' command at the end writes the changes to the disk, making the new partition available for formatting.

Once partitions are created, they must be formatted with a file system before they can be used to store data. Linux supports a wide variety of file systems, each with its own strengths and use cases. The most used file systems in modern Linux distributions include ext4, XFS, and Btrfs. The choice of file system depends on factors such as the size of the storage device, the type of data being stored, and the specific performance requirements of the system.

The *mkfs* command is used to create a new file system on a partition. For example, to create an ext4 file system on the newly created partition, an administrator would use:

 # mkfs.ext4 /dev/sdb1

```
[obert@zero2rhcsa ~]$ sudo mkfs.ext4 /dev/sdb1
[sudo] password for obert:
mke2fs 1.46.5 (30-Dec-2021)
Creating filesystem with 244224 4k blocks and 61056 inodes
Filesystem UUID: 07357148-b4f4-40d2-b779-685ad041da59
Superblock backups stored on blocks:
        32768, 98304, 163840, 229376

Allocating group tables: done
Writing inode tables: done
Creating journal (4096 blocks): done
Writing superblocks and filesystem accounting information: done

[obert@zero2rhcsa ~]$ 
```

This command formats the first partition on */dev/sdb* with the ext4 file system, preparing it for use within the Linux system.

As Linux systems grow and evolve, the need for flexible and scalable storage solutions becomes increasingly apparent. This is where Logical Volume Management (LVM) comes into play. LVM provides a layer of abstraction between physical storage devices and the file systems used by the operating system. This abstraction allows for dynamic resizing of storage volumes, easy addition or removal of physical storage, and the ability to take snapshots of logical volumes for backup purposes. LVM operates on three levels:

physical volumes (PVs),

volume groups (VGs), and

logical volumes (LVs). Physical volumes are the actual storage devices or partitions. These are combined into volume groups, which act as pools of storage. From these pools, logical volumes are created, which can be formatted with a file system and used by the operating system.

To illustrate the power of LVM, consider a scenario where you are a system administrator who needs to expand the storage capacity of a file server. Without LVM, this might require downtime to add new disks, repartition existing ones, or even migrate data to a larger storage array. With LVM, the process can be much smoother for you using the following commands:

 # pvcreate /dev/sdc

 # vgextend vg_rhcsa /dev/sdc

 # lvextend -L +20G /dev/vg_rhcsa/lv_files

 # resize2fs /dev/vg_rhcsa/lv_files

Before executing the commands above, remember a partition needs to be created with the desired size, type, and set to Linux LVM, then exit *fdisk* command process. This sequence of commands creates a new physical volume from a new disk (*/dev/sdc*), adds it to an existing volume group *(vg_rhcsa)*, extends a logical volume (lv_files) by 20GB, and finally resizes the file system to use the newly available space. All of this can be done while the system is running and without interrupting access to the existing data.

Once storage devices are partitioned, formatted, and potentially managed through LVM, they need to be integrated into the Linux file system hierarchy. This is accomplished through the process of mounting. Mounting makes the contents of a file system accessible under a specific directory in the Linux directory tree. The mount command is used to manually mount file systems, while the */etc/fstab* file is used to define file systems that should be automatically mounted at boot time.

For example, to manually mount our newly created ext4 file system, we would use:

 # mount /dev/sdb1 /mnt/rhcsa

This command mounts the first partition of /dev/sdb at the mount point /mnt/rhcsa, making its contents accessible through that directory. To make this mount persistent across reboots, an entry would be added to the /etc/fstab file:

/dev/sdb1   /mnt/rhcsa   ext4   defaults   0 2

This line instructs the system to automatically mount the specified partition at boot time.

As systems grow and multiple users share storage resources, it often becomes necessary to implement controls on storage usage to prevent any single user or group from consuming all available space. This is where disk quotas come into play. Quotas allow system administrators to set limits on the amount of disk space or number of files that can be used by individual users or groups. I did not intend to make this book voluminous, but I cannot leave certain things I believe will brooding your understanding.

So, please see some key elements of disk quotas:

Elements	Description of the Elements
User Quotas	The limit set for a user on disk usage
Group Quotas	The limits set to users because they are in a particular group
Hard Link	The cap on disk usage the user cannot exceed.
Soft Link	The threshold users can temporarily exceed due to the grace window.
Grace Period	This is when user exceed their soft limit until hitting the hard limit.

To implement quotas, the file system must first be mounted with quota options enabled. This is typically done by adding the *usrquota* and *grpquota* options to the mount command or the */etc/fstab* file. For example:

/dev/sdb1   /mnt/rhcsa   ext4   defaults,usrquota,grpquota   0 2

Once the file system is mounted with quota options, the *quotacheck* command is used to initialize the quota database:

 # quotacheck -cugv /mnt/rhcsa

This command creates user and group quota files and scans the file system to build the initial quota database.

With the quota system initialized, administrators can use the *edquota* command to set specific quotas for users or groups. For instance:

 # edquota -u obert

This command opens an editor where limits can be set for the user "*obert*" on various file systems.

Quotas can be soft limits, which allow users to temporarily exceed their allocation, or hard limits, which represent absolute maximums. By carefully setting and managing quotas, administrators can ensure the fair use of storage resources and prevent storage-related issues from impacting system stability or user productivity.

As we conclude our exploration of storage management and file systems, these concepts form a critical foundation for effective Linux administration. From the basic tasks of partitioning and formatting disks to the advanced techniques of LVM and quota management, mastering these skills is essential for maintaining a robust and efficient Linux environment. In the next chapter, we will build upon this knowledge as we delve into the intricacies of process and service management, exploring how Linux handles running programs and system services to keep your system running smoothly and efficiently.

Chapter 5:

Process and Service Management

As we delve into the intricacies of Linux system administration, it's crucial to understand how processes and services function within the operating system. This knowledge forms the backbone of effective system management and troubleshooting. In the previous chapter, we explored storage management and file systems, which provide the foundation for data storage and retrieval. Now, we'll build upon that knowledge by examining how Linux manages running programs and system services.

Understanding Linux processes is fundamental to grasping how the operating system operates. A process, in the simplest terms, is an instance of a running program. When you launch an application or execute a command, Linux creates a process to manage that task. Each process is assigned a unique Process ID (PID), which allows the system to track and manage it effectively. The concept of processes is central to the multitasking capabilities of Linux, enabling the simultaneous execution of multiple programs and tasks.

Processes in Linux can be categorized into several types based on their behavior and relationship to the user interface. Foreground processes are those that interact directly with the user through the terminal or graphical interface. These processes typically wait for user input or display output directly to the screen. On the other hand, background processes run without direct user interaction, often performing tasks in the background while the user continues with other activities. Understanding the distinction between these process types is crucial for efficient system management and resource allocation.

One of the key aspects of process management in Linux is the hierarchical relationship between processes. Every process, except for the initial system process (usually with PID 1), has a parent process. This parent-child relationship forms a tree-like structure, with the initial process at the root. When a process creates another process, it becomes the parent, and the new process is its child. This hierarchy is essential for understanding process inheritance, signal handling, and termination behavior.

To effectively manage processes, Linux provides a variety of tools and commands. The *'ps'* command is one of the most fundamental and versatile tools for viewing process information. By default, *'ps'* displays information about processes associated with the current terminal session. However, with various options, it can provide a comprehensive view of all system processes. For instance,

'ps aux' shows a detailed list of all processes running on the system, including

those of other users and system processes.

```
[obert@zero2rhcsa ~]$ ps -aux
USER        PID %CPU %MEM    VSZ   RSS TTY       STAT START    TIME COMMAND
root          1  0.1  0.5 108840 19480 ?         Ss   07:49    0:03 /usr/lib/syst
root          2  0.0  0.0      0     0 ?         S    07:49    0:00 [kthreadd]
root          3  0.0  0.0      0     0 ?         I<   07:49    0:00 [rcu_gp]
root          4  0.0  0.0      0     0 ?         I<   07:49    0:00 [rcu_par_gp]
root          5  0.0  0.0      0     0 ?         I<   07:49    0:00 [slub_flushwq
root          6  0.0  0.0      0     0 ?         I<   07:49    0:00 [netns]
```

Definition of the key columns:

Key Column	Explained
USER	Username of the process owner
PID	The unique identifier for each process
%CPU	The percentage of CPU usage
%MEM	The percentage of Memory usage
VSZ	Size of the virtual memory
RSS	The resident set size, which is the actual physical memory used by the process
TTY	The terminal the process was imitated on
STAT	This is the process stat, which could be: (R) Running, (S) Sleeping, (T) Stopped. (Z) Zombie

TIME	Total amount of CPU time consumed by process
COMMAND	The command that started the process. For example: ps –aux There is also a process ID for the command used to view the process ID of other commands and system resources.

Another invaluable tool for process management is the *'top'* command. Unlike *'ps'*, which provides a static snapshot of processes, *'top'* offers a real-time, dynamic view of the system's processes. It displays a continuously updated list of the most CPU-intensive processes and system-wide statistics such as CPU usage, memory utilization, and load averages. The *'top'* command is handy for identifying resource-hungry processes and monitoring system performance over time. For example, let's look at the real-time view of the zero2rhcsa system's processes:

```
[obert@zero2rhcsa ~]$ top

top - 08:26:11 up 36 min,  2 users,  load average: 0.02, 0.05, 0.08
Tasks: 234 total,   1 running, 233 sleeping,   0 stopped,   0 zombie
%Cpu(s):  0.2 us,  0.2 sy,  0.0 ni, 99.5 id,  0.0 wa,  0.0 hi,  0.2 si,  0.0 st
MiB Mem :   3659.7 total,    1984.1 free,    1213.9 used,    706.1 buff/cache
MiB Swap:  19072.0 total,   19072.0 free,       0.0 used.   2445.9 avail Mem

    PID USER       PR  NI    VIRT    RES    SHR S  %CPU  %MEM     TIME+ COMMAND
   5522 obert      20   0 4000896 333536 121292 S   0.7   8.9   0:27.00 gnome-s+
   5775 obert      20   0  610180  20328  14080 S   0.3   0.5   0:00.38 gsd-sma+
   5982 root       20   0  376304  58440  26880 S   0.3   1.6   0:01.27 rhsm-se+
   6601 root       20   0       0      0      0 I   0.3   0.0   0:00.63 kworker+
   6794 obert      20   0  226056   4352   3456 R   0.3   0.1   0:00.21 top
      1 root       20   0  108840  17984  10668 S   0.0   0.5   0:03.48 systemd
      2 root       20   0       0      0      0 S   0.0   0.0   0:00.04 kthreadd
```

When it comes to controlling processes, Linux provides several mechanisms. The *'kill'* command is used to send signals to processes, allowing administrators to terminate, pause, or manipulate running programs. While *'kill'* is often associated with forcefully ending processes, it's capable of sending various signals beyond just termination. For example, *'kill -STOP'* can pause a process without termination, while *'kill -CONT'* can resume a paused process. Understanding these signals and their effects is crucial for fine-grained process control and troubleshooting. For example, let us consider you are running a CPU-intensive job with process ID 4321. You can temporarily free up that space and resume that job later without losing the state of the job with the following commands:

 # kill – STOP <PID>   # kill – STOP 4321... pause process

 # kill – CONT <PID> # kill – CONT 4321... resume process

Process priorities in Linux are managed through the *'nice'* system. Every process has a niceness value, ranging from -20 (highest priority) to 19 (lowest priority). The *'nice'* command allows you to start a process with a modified niceness value, while *'renice'* can adjust the priority of an already running process. This system enables administrators to allocate CPU resources more efficiently, ensuring that critical processes receive the necessary computational power while less important tasks are given lower priority. The syntax to start a new process with a desired priority is as follows:

 # nice -n <priority> <the new process>

Consider the new process to be an important script, such as a script for patching the server; let's call the script patchin.sh. Running this script with a specified PID is as follows:

 # nice –n 8 patchin.sh

The script now runs with a nice value of 8, just how I want it to.

As we transition from individual processes to system-wide services, we encounter the concept of service management. In modern Linux distributions, including Red Hat Enterprise Linux, service management is primarily handled by systemd. Systemd is an init system and system manager that has become the de facto standard in many Linux distributions. It is responsible for initializing the system during boot, managing system processes and services, and handling system shutdown.

Systemd introduces the concept of units, which are resources that the system knows how to manage. The most common type of unit is a *service unit,* which describes how to manage a service or application on the system. Other unit types include *mount units* for managing mount points and *timer units* for scheduling tasks similar to cron jobs.

The primary tool for interacting with systemd is the *'systemctl'* command. This versatile command allows administrators to *start, stop, restart,* and *check* the status of services. For example,

systemctl start httpd would start the Apache web server, while

systemctl status sshd would display the current status of the SSH daemon. The *'systemctl'* command also provides options for enabling or disabling services at boot time, making it easy to configure which services should automatically start when the system boots up. Lets us look at the Apache web server running on zero2rhcsa vm.

```
[obert@zero2rhcsa ~]$ systemctl stop sshd
[obert@zero2rhcsa ~]$ systemctl status sshd
○ sshd.service - OpenSSH server daemon
     Loaded: loaded (/usr/lib/systemd/system/sshd.service; enabled; preset: ena>
     Active: inactive (dead) since Mon 2024-11-04 09:44:10 CST; 9s ago
   Duration: 1h 54min 11.774s
       Docs: man:sshd(8)
             man:sshd_config(5)
    Process: 1188 ExecStart=/usr/sbin/sshd -D $OPTIONS (code=exited, status=0/S>
   Main PID: 1188 (code=exited, status=0/SUCCESS)
        CPU: 66ms

Nov 04 07:49:58 zero2rhcsa systemd[1]: Starting OpenSSH server daemon...
Nov 04 07:49:58 zero2rhcsa sshd[1188]: Server listening on 0.0.0.0 port 22.
Nov 04 07:49:58 zero2rhcsa systemd[1]: Started OpenSSH server daemon.
Nov 04 07:49:58 zero2rhcsa sshd[1188]: Server listening on :: port 22.
Nov 04 09:44:10 zero2rhcsa systemd[1]: Stopping OpenSSH server daemon...
Nov 04 09:44:10 zero2rhcsa sshd[1188]: Received signal 15; terminating.
Nov 04 09:44:10 zero2rhcsa systemd[1]: sshd.service: Deactivated successfully.
Nov 04 09:44:10 zero2rhcsa systemd[1]: Stopped OpenSSH server daemon.
lines 1-18/18 (END)
```

```
[obert@zero2rhcsa ~]$ systemctl start sshd
[obert@zero2rhcsa ~]$ systemctl status sshd
● sshd.service - OpenSSH server daemon
     Loaded: loaded (/usr/lib/systemd/system/sshd.service; enabled; preset: ena>
     Active: active (running) since Mon 2024-11-04 09:49:14 CST; 5s ago
       Docs: man:sshd(8)
             man:sshd_config(5)
   Main PID: 11014 (sshd)
      Tasks: 1 (limit: 23016)
     Memory: 1.4M
        CPU: 11ms
     CGroup: /system.slice/sshd.service
             └─11014 "sshd: /usr/sbin/sshd -D [listener] 0 of 10-100 startups"

Nov 04 09:49:14 zero2rhcsa systemd[1]: Starting OpenSSH server daemon...
Nov 04 09:49:14 zero2rhcsa sshd[11014]: Server listening on 0.0.0.0 port 22.
Nov 04 09:49:14 zero2rhcsa sshd[11014]: Server listening on :: port 22.
Nov 04 09:49:14 zero2rhcsa systemd[1]: Started OpenSSH server daemon.
lines 1-16/16 (END)
```

One of the significant advantages of systemd is its ability to manage

dependencies between services. When a service is started, Systemd automatically starts any other services that it depends on. How cool is that? This dependency

management ensures that services are started in the correct order and that all

necessary components are running before a service becomes active. For instance, a

web application service might depend on both a database service and a web server

service. Systemd would ensure that these dependencies are satisfied before starting

the web application service.

Systemd also provides powerful logging capabilities through its journal. The

'journalctl' command allows administrators to view and query system logs,

including those generated by systemd-managed services. This centralized logging

system simplifies the process of troubleshooting service-related issues and

monitoring system events. The journal can be filtered by various criteria, such as

time range, service name, or severity level, making it an invaluable tool for system

analysis and debugging. # *journalctl* without any option.

Configuring system startup and shutdown procedures is another crucial aspect of service management. Systemd uses target units to define system states, similar to runlevels in older init systems. The default target determines which services and resources are activated during system boot. Administrators can modify the default target or switch between targets to change the system's operational state. For example, switching to the rescue target would boot the system into a minimal environment for maintenance or recovery purposes.

Understanding how to manage the boot process is essential for troubleshooting and system recovery. Systemd provides tools like *systemd-analyze'* to examine the boot process and identify potential bottlenecks. This command can generate a detailed report of how long each service took to start during boot, helping administrators optimize the startup sequence and reduce boot times. Let us see how long it took some services on my zero2rhcsa server during boot:

```
[obert@zero2rhcsa ~]$ systemd-analyze
Startup finished in 2.745s (kernel) + 6.441s (initrd) + 27.118s (userspace) = 36.305s
graphical.target reached after 26.714s in userspace.
[obert@zero2rhcsa ~]$
```

In addition to managing regular services, systemd also handles socket activation, a feature that allows services to be started on-demand when a client attempts to connect to their associated socket. This approach can improve system performance and resource utilization by avoiding the need to keep rarely-used services running continuously.

As we conclude our exploration of process and service management, it's clear that these concepts are fundamental to effective Linux system administration. The ability to monitor, control, and optimize processes and services is crucial for maintaining system performance, stability, and security. In the next chapter, we'll build upon this knowledge as we delve into networking fundamentals, exploring how Linux systems communicate and interact within networks. Understanding network configuration and troubleshooting will complement your skills in process and service management, further enhancing your capabilities as a Linux administrator.

Chapter 6:
Networking Fundamentals

As we delve into the realm of networking fundamentals, it's crucial to understand how the previous chapter's focus on process and service management relates to our current topic. Many of the services we learned to manage are network-related, and understanding the underlying networking principles will enhance our ability to configure and troubleshoot these services effectively.

TCP/IP basics form the foundation of modern networking, and as Linux administrators, we must have a firm grasp of these concepts. The Transmission Control Protocol (TCP) and Internet Protocol (IP) work in tandem to ensure reliable data transmission across networks. TCP operates at the transport layer of the OSI model, providing ordered, error-checked delivery of data packets. IP, on the other hand, functions at the network layer, handling the addressing and routing of these packets.

To truly appreciate the significance of TCP/IP, we must consider its historical context. Developed in the 1970s by Vint Cerf and Bob Kahn, TCP/IP was designed to be robust and adaptable, capable of surviving partial network failures. This resilience has contributed to its longevity and widespread adoption. As noted by Andrew S. Tanenbaum in his book "Computer Networks," "The Internet protocol suite was carefully designed to work in a diverse environment, from slow links to high-speed networks, and to be independent of any particular hardware technology."

In the Linux environment, understanding TCP/IP is paramount for effective system administration. The kernel's networking stack implements these protocols, allowing for seamless communication between your Linux system and other devices on the network. This implementation is highly efficient and configurable, giving administrators fine-grained control over network behavior.

When working with TCP/IP on Linux systems, we often interact with the protocol suite through various tools and configuration files. The *'/etc/protocols'* file, for instance, maps protocol names to their corresponding numbers. Familiarity with this file can be helpful when troubleshooting network issues or configuring firewalls.

Moving beyond the theoretical aspects of TCP/IP, let's explore the practical side of configuring network interfaces on Linux systems. Network interface configuration is a fundamental skill for any Linux administrator, as it forms the basis for all network communication.

In modern Linux distributions, particularly those based on Red Hat Enterprise Linux (RHEL), network interfaces are typically managed using NetworkManager. This powerful daemon provides a high-level interface for configuring network connections. However, it's essential to understand the underlying configuration files and commands, as they offer more granular control and are crucial in scenarios where NetworkManager may not be available or appropriate.

The primary configuration file for network interfaces on RHEL-based systems is *'/etc/sysconfig/network-scripts/ifcfg-<interface_name>'*. This file contains various parameters that define the behavior of a network interface. For example, to configure a static IP address for an Ethernet interface named 'eth0', you might create a file named 'ifcfg-eth0' with contents similar to the following:

DEVICE=eth0

BOOTPROTO=static

IPADDR=192.168.10.100

NETMASK=255.255.255.0

GATEWAY=192.168.10.1

ONBOOT=yes

This configuration sets a static IP address of *192.168.10.100* with a subnet mask of *255.255.255.0* and a gateway of *192.168.10.1* on interface *eth0*. The *'ONBOOT=yes'* parameter ensures that this interface is activated when the system boots.

While editing configuration files directly is powerful, it's often more convenient to use command-line tools for network configuration. The *'ip'* command, which is part of the iproute2 package, is a versatile tool for viewing and manipulating network interfaces and routing tables. For instance, to view the current IP addresses assigned to all interfaces, you would use:

 # ip addr show

To add a new IP address to an interface, you might use:

 # ip addr add 192.168.10.101/24 dev eth0

This command adds the IP address *192.168.10.101* with a 24-bit subnet mask to the eth0 interface.

It's worth noting that while these changes take effect immediately, they are not persistent across reboots unless saved to the appropriate configuration files. This temporary nature can be advantageous for testing configurations before committing them permanently.

As we progress in our networking journey, we encounter the critical concepts of DNS (Domain Name System) and hostname resolution. DNS acts as the internet's phonebook, translating human-readable domain names into IP addresses that computers can understand. This system is fundamental to the functioning of the internet and most internal networks.

In Linux systems, DNS configuration primarily involves the '/etc/resolv.conf' file. This file specifies the IP addresses of DNS servers that the system should query when resolving domain names. A typical '/etc/resolv.conf' might look like this:

nameserver 8.8.8.8

nameserver 8.8.4.4

These entries would configure the system to use Google's public DNS servers. However, it's important to note that on many modern systems, this file is managed dynamically by NetworkManager or systemd-resolved, and manual edits may be overwritten.

For local hostname resolution, Linux systems use the '/etc/hosts' file. This file allows you to map IP addresses to hostnames, which can be useful for creating shortcuts or overriding DNS for specific hosts. A basic '/etc/hosts' file might contain:

127.0.0.1   localhost

::1   localhost

192.168.10.10   myserver.local myserver

This configuration ensures that 'localhost' resolves to the loopback address (both IPv4 and IPv6) and that 'myserver.local' and 'myserver' resolve to 192.168.10.10.

Understanding these files and their purposes is crucial for effective network administration. As noted by Evi Nemeth in the book "UNIX and Linux System Administration Handbook," "The separation of /etc/hosts and DNS creates a two-level naming system that's simple yet powerful. Local information in /etc/hosts can override information in DNS, and local names need not be published to the world at large."

As we delve deeper into networking, troubleshooting becomes an increasingly important skill. Network issues can arise from a myriad of sources, from misconfigured interfaces to DNS problems and from routing issues to physical layer failures. Developing a systematic approach to troubleshooting is essential for any Linux administrator.

One of the first tools in any network troubleshooter's arsenal is the 'ping' command. This simple yet powerful utility sends ICMP echo request packets to a specified host and listens for responses. For example:

ping google.com

This command will continuously ping google.com, providing information about packet loss and round-trip times. If this fails, it could indicate issues with DNS resolution, routing, or connectivity at various levels of the network stack.

For more detailed analysis of the route that packets take to reach a destination, the 'traceroute' command is invaluable. It shows the path of packets through the network, revealing potential bottlenecks or points of failure. For instance:

traceroute google.com

This command will display each hop that packets take on their journey to Google's servers, along with the time taken for each hop.

When dealing with DNS issues, the *'dig'* command (Domain Information Groper) is an essential tool. It provides a flexible way to query DNS servers and can be invaluable in diagnosing DNS-related problems. For example:

 # dig google.com

This command will return detailed information about the DNS records for google.com, including the authoritative name servers and IP addresses associated with the domain.

```
[obert@zero2rhcsa ~]$ dig google.com

; <<>> DiG 9.16.23-RH <<>> google.com
;; global options: +cmd
;; Got answer:
;; ->>HEADER<<- opcode: QUERY, status: NOERROR, id: 6787
;; flags: qr rd ra; QUERY: 1, ANSWER: 6, AUTHORITY: 0, ADDITIONAL: 1

;; OPT PSEUDOSECTION:
; EDNS: version: 0, flags:; udp: 4096
;; QUESTION SECTION:
;google.com.                    IN      A

;; ANSWER SECTION:
google.com.             81      IN      A       142.251.116.113
google.com.             81      IN      A       142.251.116.139
google.com.             81      IN      A       142.251.116.102
google.com.             81      IN      A       142.251.116.101
google.com.             81      IN      A       142.251.116.100
google.com.             81      IN      A       142.251.116.138

;; Query time: 5 msec
;; SERVER: 192.168.1.254#53(192.168.1.254)
;; WHEN: Sat Nov 09 11:56:45 CST 2024
;; MSG SIZE  rcvd: 135

[obert@zero2rhcsa ~]$
```

For more complex network analysis, tools like *'tcpdump'* and *'Wireshark'*
allow administrators to capture and analyze network traffic at a packet level. While
these tools have a steeper learning curve, they provide unparalleled insight into
network behavior and can be crucial for diagnosing subtle or intermittent issues.

```
[obert@zero2rhcsa ~]$ sudo tcpdump
[sudo] password for obert:
dropped privs to tcpdump
tcpdump: verbose output suppressed, use -v[v]... for full protocol decode
listening on enp0s3, link-type EN10MB (Ethernet), snapshot length 262144 bytes
```

As we conclude our exploration of networking fundamentals, it's important to recognize that this field is vast and constantly evolving. The concepts and tools we've discussed form a solid foundation, but continuous learning and adaptation are necessary to stay current in the fast-paced world of network administration.

In the next chapter, we'll build upon this networking knowledge as we delve into package management and software installation. Understanding network fundamentals is crucial for effectively managing software repositories, downloading packages, and resolving dependencies. The ability to configure and troubleshoot network connections will prove invaluable as we explore the intricacies of managing software on Linux systems.

Chapter 7:

Package Management and Software Installation

As we transition from our discussion on networking fundamentals, it's essential to understand how software is managed and installed on Linux systems. This chapter delves into the intricacies of package management and software installation, crucial skills for any Linux administrator aiming to maintain a stable and up-to-date system.

At the heart of Linux software management are package managers, sophisticated tools designed to streamline the process of installing, updating, and removing software. In the Red Hat ecosystem, two primary package managers stand out: *YUM (Yellowdog Updater Modified)* and its more recent successor, *DNF (Dandified YUM)*. These tools not only handle the installation of software but also manage dependencies, ensuring that all required libraries and components are present on the system.

YUM has been the cornerstone of Red Hat package management for many years. Its intuitive command-line interface and robust functionality have made it a favorite among system administrators. To install a package using YUM, one simply needs to execute a command like

 # yum install package_name

This seemingly simple command triggers a complex series of operations: *YUM* queries configured repositories, resolves dependencies, downloads necessary packages, and installs them in the correct order. Let's install the tool Git, a distributed version control system used to control source code and file versions. But we need to check whether Git is already installed or not using the command:

 # rpm -q packagename = rpm -q git... then we shall install, not already installed.

```
complete:
[root@zero2rhcsa yum.repos.d]# rpm -q git
package git is not installed
[root@zero2rhcsa yum.repos.d]#
```

```
[root@zero2rhcsa yum.repos.d]# dnf install git
Updating Subscription Management repositories.
Last metadata expiration check: 0:16:38 ago on Sat 09 Nov 2024 02:16:56 PM CST.
Dependencies resolved.
==========================================================================================
 Package              Arch       Version             Repository                        Size
==========================================================================================
Installing:
 git                  x86_64     2.43.5-1.el9_4      rhel-9-for-x86_64-appstream-rpms   54 k
Installing dependencies:
 git-core-doc         noarch     2.43.5-1.el9_4      rhel-9-for-x86_64-appstream-rpms   2.9 M
 perl-Git             noarch     2.43.5-1.el9_4      rhel-9-for-x86_64-appstream-rpms   39 k
 perl-TermReadKey     x86_64     2.38-11.el9         rhel-9-for-x86_64-appstream-rpms   40 k

Transaction Summary
==========================================================================================
Install  4 Packages

Total download size: 3.1 M
Installed size: 17 M
Is this ok [y/N]: y
Downloading Packages:
(1/4): git-2.43.5-1.el9_4.x86_64.rpm                      252 kB/s |  54 kB    00:00
(2/4): perl-TermReadKey-2.38-11.el9_4.x86_64.rpm          175 kB/s |  40 kB    00:00
(3/4): perl-Git-2.43.5-1.el9_4.noarch.rpm                 539 kB/s |  39 kB    00:00
(4/4): git-core-doc-2.43.5-1.el9_4.noarch.rpm             9.4 MB/s | 2.9 MB    00:00
------------------------------------------------------------------------------------------
Total                                                     9.6 MB/s | 3.1 MB    00:00
Running transaction check
Transaction check succeeded.
Running transaction test
Transaction test succeeded.
Running transaction
  Preparing        :                                                            1/1
  Installing       : git-core-doc-2.43.5-1.el9_4.noarch                         1/4
  Installing       : perl-TermReadKey-2.38-11.el9_4.x86_64                      2/4
  Installing       : perl-Git-2.43.5-1.el9_4.noarch                             3/4
  Installing       : git-2.43.5-1.el9_4.x86_64                                  4/4
  Running scriptlet: git-2.43.5-1.el9_4.x86_64                                  4/4
  Verifying        : perl-TermReadKey-2.38-11.el9_4.x86_64                      1/4
  Verifying        : git-2.43.5-1.el9_4.x86_64                                  2/4
  Verifying        : git-core-doc-2.43.5-1.el9_4.noarch                         3/4
  Verifying        : perl-Git-2.43.5-1.el9_4.noarch                             4/4
Installed products updated.

Installed:
  git-2.43.5-1.el9_4.x86_64                   git-core-doc-2.43.5-1.el9_4.noarch
```

However, as with all technology, evolution is inevitable. Ladies and gentlemen, with pleasure, I present *DNF,* the next-generation package manager designed to address some of *YUM's* limitations while maintaining backward compatibility. *DNF* boasts improved performance, especially in dependency resolution, and introduces new features like better error reporting and enhanced integration with system plugins.

One of the key strengths of both *YUM* and *DNF* is their ability to manage software repositories. Repositories are centralized collections of packages, typically maintained by distribution vendors or third-party organizations. By default, Red Hat Enterprise Linux systems are configured to use official Red Hat repositories, ensuring that all software comes from a trusted source and is compatible with the system.

Managing repositories is a critical skill for system administrators. It involves not only knowing how to add or remove repositories but also understanding the implications of using different sources. For instance, enabling third-party repositories can provide access to a wider range of software but may introduce compatibility issues or security risks if not properly vetted.

To add a new repository, administrators typically create a .repo file in the */etc/yum.repos.d/* directory. This file contains crucial information such as the repository's name, base URL, and whether it should be enabled by default. For example, to add the EPEL (Extra Packages for Enterprise Linux) repository, one might create a file named epel.repo with contents similar to:

[epel]

name=Extra Packages for Enterprise Linux 7 - $basearch

baseurl=http://download.fedoraproject.org/pub/epel/7/$basearch

enabled=1

gpgcheck=1

gpgkey=file:///etc/pki/rpm-gpg/RPM-GPG-KEY-EPEL-7

This configuration not only adds the repository but also ensures that package signatures are checked for authenticity, a crucial security measure.

While *YUM* and *DNF* handle the majority of software installation needs, there are times when compiling software from source becomes necessary. This might be due to the need for customized builds, the absence of a package in standard repositories, or simply for learning purposes.

Compiling from source is a more involved process that typically follows a standard sequence:

configure,

make, and

make install. The "configure" step checks the system for necessary dependencies and creates a Makefile tailored to the local environment. The *"make"* command then compiles the source code into binary form, and finally, *"make install"* places the compiled files in the appropriate system directories.

For example, to compile and install a hypothetical software package named *"myapp"*, one might follow these steps:

./configure

make

sudo make install

This process, while more complex than using a package manager, offers unparalleled flexibility in terms of customization and optimization.

It's worth noting that compiling from source can introduce challenges in terms of system management. Unlike packages installed via *YUM* or *DNF*, software compiled from source isn't tracked by the package management system, making updates and removal more complicated. For this reason, tools like *checkinstall* have been developed to create basic packages from compiled sources, allowing for easier management.

As we delve deeper into package management, it's crucial to understand the concept of dependencies. Software rarely exists in isolation; most programs rely on shared libraries and other software components to function. Package managers excel at resolving these dependencies automatically, ensuring that all necessary components are installed alongside the requested software.

However, dependency resolution can sometimes lead to conflicts, especially when dealing with complex software stacks or multiple repositories. In such cases, administrators may need to manually intervene, either by specifying version constraints or by carefully managing the order of installations.

Another critical aspect of package management is keeping the system up-to-date. Regular updates are essential for maintaining system security and stability. Both *YUM* and *DNF* provide simple commands for updating all installed packages:

sudo yum update

or

sudo dnf upgrade

These commands not only update existing packages but also install any new dependencies that might have been introduced. It's generally recommended to review the proposed changes before confirming the update, especially on production systems where unexpected changes could impact service availability.

For more granular control, administrators can choose to update specific packages or exclude certain packages from updates. This level of control is particularly important in environments where certain software versions must be maintained for compatibility reasons.

As we conclude our exploration of package management and software installation, it's clear that these skills form a cornerstone of effective system administration. The ability to efficiently manage software, from installation and updates to removal and dependency resolution, is crucial for maintaining secure, stable, and functional Linux systems.

In the next chapter, we'll build upon this foundation by delving into system security and access control. We'll explore how to implement firewalls, configure SELinux, secure SSH access, and audit system security. These topics will further enhance your ability to maintain robust and secure Linux environments, complementing the software management skills we've discussed here.

Chapter 8:

System Security and Access Control

As we transition from package management and software installation, we now turn our attention to a critical aspect of Linux system administration: security and access control. In today's interconnected world, protecting your systems from unauthorized access and potential threats is paramount. This chapter will delve into the essential tools and techniques used in Red Hat Enterprise Linux to secure your systems effectively.

Implementing firewalls with *firewalld* is our first line of defense in system security. Firewalld is a dynamic firewall manager that provides a powerful yet user-friendly interface for configuring network traffic rules. Unlike its predecessor, *iptables, firewalld* offers a more flexible and easier-to-manage approach to firewall configuration. At its core, *firewalld* uses zones to define the level of trust for network connections. Each zone can have its own set of rules, allowing administrators to create complex security policies with relative ease.

To begin working with *firewalld*, we first need to ensure that the service is running. This can be done using the *systemctl* command:

sudo systemctl start firewalld

sudo systemctl enable firewalld

```
[root@zero2rhcsa yum.repos.d]# cd
[root@zero2rhcsa ~]# systemctl status firewalld.service
• firewalld.service - firewalld - dynamic firewall daemon
   Loaded: loaded (/usr/lib/systemd/system/firewalld.service; enabled; preset: enabled)
   Active: active (running) since Sat 2024-11-09 09:44:01 CST; 5h 5min ago
     Docs: man:firewalld(1)
 Main PID: 1038 (firewalld)
    Tasks: 4 (limit: 23016)
   Memory: 43.4M
      CPU: 2.894s
   CGroup: /system.slice/firewalld.service
           └─1038 /usr/bin/python3 -s /usr/sbin/firewalld --nofork --nopid

Nov 09 09:44:00 zero2rhcsa systemd[1]: Starting firewalld - dynamic firewall daemon...
Nov 09 09:44:01 zero2rhcsa systemd[1]: Started firewalld - dynamic firewall daemon.
```

Once *firewalld* is active, we can start configuring our firewall rules. The

primary tool for interacting with *firewalld* is the *firewall-cmd* command. For

instance, to list all the available zones, we can use:

firewall-cmd --get-zones

```
[root@zero2rhcsa ~]# firewall-cmd --get-zones
block dmz drop external home internal libvirt libvirt-routed nm-shared public trusted work
[root@zero2rhcsa ~]# █
```

This will display a list of predefined zones such as drop, block, public, and

trusted. Each zone represents a different level of trust and has its own default set of

rules. The public zone, for example, is typically used for public networks where

you don't trust other computers but still want to allow selected incoming

connections.

To view the current active zone, we can use:

firewall-cmd --get-active-zones

```
[root@zero2rhcsa ~]# firewall-cmd --get-active-zones
public
  interfaces: enp0s3
[root@zero2rhcsa ~]#
```

This will show which zone is currently active on each network interface. By default, the public zone is often the active zone.

One of the most common tasks in firewall management is opening ports for specific services. For example, if we want to allow incoming SSH connections, we need to open port 22. We can do this with the following command:

sudo firewall-cmd --zone=public --add-service=ssh --permanent

This command adds the SSH service to the public zone permanently. The *--permanent* option ensures that the rule persists across reboots. After making changes, we need to reload the firewall for the changes to take effect:

sudo firewall-cmd --reload

Firewalld also allow for more granular control. Instead of opening an entire service, we can open specific ports:

sudo firewall-cmd --zone=public --add-port=8080/tcp --permanent

This command opens TCP port 8080 in the public zone. Remember to always reload the firewall after making changes.

While *firewalld* provides excellent network-level security, Red Hat Enterprise Linux also includes a powerful tool for system-level access control: SELinux (Security-Enhanced Linux). SELinux is a mandatory access control (MAC) system built into the Linux kernel. It provides an additional layer of security beyond the traditional discretionary access control (DAC) implemented through file permissions.

SELinux operates on the principle of least privilege, where processes are given only the minimum level of access required to function. This significantly reduces the potential damage that could be caused by a compromised process. SELinux uses security contexts to define access permissions. Every process, file, and system object has a security context, which is used to determine whether access should be granted or denied.

By default, SELinux is enabled on Red Hat Enterprise Linux systems. You can check its status using the following command:

getenforce

This will return one of three possible states: Enforcing, Permissive, or Disabled. In Enforcing mode, the SELinux policy is enforced and access is denied for unauthorized actions. In Permissive mode, SELinux logs policy violations but does not enforce them. Disabled mode turns off SELinux completely.

While SELinux provides robust security, it can sometimes interfere with the normal operation of applications, especially those not designed with SELinux in mind. When troubleshooting SELinux-related issues, the first step is often to check the SELinux logs. The audit log (/var/log/audit/audit.log), is a massive file containing detailed information about SELinux policy violations.

For easier analysis of SELinux issues, Red Hat provides the *sealert* tool. This tool can be used to generate user-friendly explanations of SELinux denials and suggest possible solutions. To use *sealert,* you first need to install the setroubleshoot-server package:

sudo yum install setroubleshoot-server

Then, you can analyze recent SELinux alerts with:

sealert -a /var/log/audit/audit.log

```
[root@zero2rhcsa audit]# sealert -a /var/log/audit/audit.log
100% done
found 0 alerts in /var/log/audit/audit.log
[root@zero2rhcsa audit]# dnf install setroubleshoot-server
Updating Subscription Management repositories.
Last metadata expiration check: 0:53:08 ago on Sat 09 Nov 2024 02:16:56 PM CST.
Package setroubleshoot-server-3.3.32-1.el9.x86_64 is already installed.
Dependencies resolved.
Nothing to do.
Complete!
[root@zero2rhcsa audit]# sealert -a /var/log/audit/audit.log
100% done
found 0 alerts in /var/log/audit/audit.log
[root@zero2rhcsa audit]#
```

This will provide a detailed breakdown of recent SELinux denials and potential solutions.

While SELinux is a powerful tool, it's important to note that it should not be disabled unless absolutely necessary. Many system administrators, frustrated by SELinux denials, are tempted to disable it entirely. However, this significantly reduces the security of the system. Instead, it's better to take the time to understand and properly configure SELinux policies.

Moving on to another crucial aspect of system security, we need to discuss securing SSH access. SSH (Secure Shell) is the primary method for remote access to Linux systems, and as such, it's a common target for attackers. Properly securing SSH is essential for maintaining the overall security of your system.

The first step in securing SSH is to ensure that you're using the latest version of OpenSSH. You can check your current version with:

ssh -V

If you're not running the latest version, update your system to get the most recent security patches.

Next, it's important to configure SSH to use only secure protocols and ciphers. Edit the SSH configuration file (/etc/ssh/sshd_config) and ensure the following lines are present and uncommented:

Protocol 2

HostKey /etc/ssh/ssh_host_rsa_key

HostKey /etc/ssh/ssh_host_ecdsa_key

HostKey /etc/ssh/ssh_host_ed25519_key

KexAlgorithms

curve25519-sha256@libssh.org,ecdh-sha2-nistp521,ecdh-sha2-nistp384,ecd

h-sha2-nistp256,diffie-hellman-group-exchange-sha256

Ciphers

chacha20-poly1305@openssh.com,aes256-gcm@openssh.com,aes128-gcm

@openssh.com,aes256-ctr,aes192-ctr,aes128-ctr

MACs:

hmac-sha2-512-etm@openssh.com,hmac-sha2-256-etm@openssh.com,umac
-128-etm@openssh.com

These settings ensure that only secure, modern protocols and ciphers are used for SSH connections.

Another important security measure is to disable root login over SSH. Add or modify the following line in the SSH configuration file:

PermitRootLogin no

This prevents direct root login via SSH, forcing users to log in as regular user and then use *sudo* for privileged operations. This adds an extra layer of security, as an attacker would need to compromise both a user account and the *sudo* mechanism to gain root access.

It's also a good practice to limit SSH access to specific users or groups. You can do this by adding the following lines to the SSH configuration file:

AllowUsers user1 user2

AllowGroups sshusers

This restricts SSH access to only the specified users or members of the specified groups.

Finally, consider implementing key-based authentication instead of password authentication. Key-based authentication is more secure and resistant to brute-force attacks. To set this up, generate an SSH key pair on your client machine:

ssh-keygen -t rsa -b 4096

Then, copy the public key to the server:

ssh-copy-id user@server

Once the key is in place, you can disable password authentication in the SSH configuration file:

PasswordAuthentication no

Remember to restart the SSH service after making any changes to the configuration file:

sudo systemctl restart sshd

The final aspect of system security we'll discuss in this chapter is auditing. Auditing is crucial for maintaining the security and integrity of your system. It allows you to track system events, detect potential security breaches, and ensure compliance with security policies.

Red Hat Enterprise Linux includes the Linux Audit system, which provides a way to track security-relevant information on your system. The audit system can track various types of events, including system calls, file accesses, and user logins.

To start using the audit system, first ensure that the *auditd* service is running:

sudo systemctl start auditd

sudo systemctl enable auditd

```
[obert@zero2rhcsa-mrsa-com etc]$ sudo systemctl status auditd.service
[sudo] password for obert:
● auditd.service - Security Auditing Service
     Loaded: loaded (/usr/lib/systemd/system/auditd.service; enabled; preset: e
     Active: active (running) since Tue 2024-11-12 00:40:50 CST; 8h ago
       Docs: man:auditd(8)
             https://github.com/linux-audit/audit-documentation
    Process: 956 ExecStart=/sbin/auditd (code=exited, status=0/SUCCESS)
    Process: 964 ExecStartPost=/sbin/augenrules --load (code=exited, status=0/S
   Main PID: 959 (auditd)
      Tasks: 4 (limit: 23030)
     Memory: 1.9M
        CPU: 556ms
     CGroup: /system.slice/auditd.service
             ├─959 /sbin/auditd
             └─961 /usr/sbin/sedispatch
```

The main configuration file for the audit system is */etc/audit/auditd.conf.* This file controls various aspects of the audit system, such as log file location, maximum log file size, and what to do when the log files are full.

To add audit rules, you can edit the *etc/audit/rules.d/audit.rules* file. For example, to audit all attempts to access a specific file, you could add the following rule:

-w /path/to/important/file -p warx -k important_file_access

Assuming we need to monitor the /etc directory:

sudo vim /etc/audit.rules.d/audit.rules

*Add the rule: **-w /etc -p warx -k etc_directory_monitor***

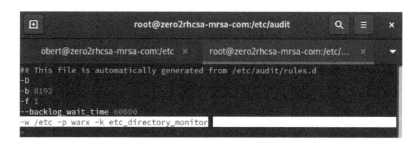

Explanation:

*-w /path/to/important/file: This specifies the **watch** path and indicates which files or directories are being monitored.*

-p warx: This defines the types of access being monitored where:

w: is write access (e.g file modifications)

a: Attribute changes (e.g permissions and ownership)

r: read access

x: execute access (e.g running script files)

-k etc_directory_monitor: is just a custom identifier for the rule in the case you need to search specific audit log entries related to it.

This rule will log all read, write, execute, and attribute change attempts on the specified file with the key "important_file_access".

To audit all sudo commands, you could add:

-w /usr/bin/sudo -p x -k sudo_usage

This will log all executions of sudo.

After adding or modifying rules, you need to reload the audit rules:

sudo auditctl -R /etc/audit/rules.d/audit.rules

To view the audit logs, you can use the *ausearch* command. For example, to view all sudo usage events:

sudo ausearch -k sudo_usage

Regular review of audit logs is an important part of maintaining system security. Consider setting up automated alerts for specific types of audit events to help you quickly respond to potential security issues.

As we conclude our discussion on system security and access control, it's important to remember that security is not a one-time setup but an ongoing process. Regularly updating your system, reviewing logs, and adjusting security policies are all crucial parts of maintaining a secure Linux environment. In the next chapter, we'll delve into system monitoring and logging, which are closely related to the security practices we've discussed here. We'll explore how to set up comprehensive logging systems and use various tools to monitor system performance and health, further enhancing your ability to maintain secure and efficient Linux systems.

Chapter 9:

System Monitoring and Logging

As we transition from the realm of system security and access control, we now delve into the equally critical domain of system monitoring and logging. In the ever-evolving landscape of Linux administration, the ability to keep a vigilant eye on system performance and maintain comprehensive logs is paramount. This chapter will equip you with the knowledge and tools necessary to effectively monitor your Linux systems and make sense of the vast amount of log data they generate.

Configuring system logging is the foundation of effective system monitoring. In Linux, the syslog protocol has long been the standard for system logging, with rsyslog (rocket-fast system for log processing) being the most widely used implementation in modern distributions, including Red Hat Enterprise Linux. The rsyslog daemon is responsible for collecting, processing, and storing log messages from various system components and applications.

To begin configuring rsyslog, we need to understand its configuration file, typically located at */etc/rsyslog.conf*. This file contains directives that determine how log messages are processed and where they are stored. Let's examine a typical

rsyslog.conf file:

```
#### RULES ####

# Log all kernel messages to the console.
# Logging much else clutters up the screen.
#kern.*                                          /dev/console

# Log anything (except mail) of level info or higher.
# Don't log private authentication messages!
*.info;mail.none;authpriv.none;cron.none        /var/log/messages

# The authpriv file has restricted access.
authpriv.*                                       /var/log/secure

# Log all the mail messages in one place.
mail.*                                          -/var/log/maillog

# Log cron stuff
cron.*                                           /var/log/cron

# Everybody gets emergency messages
*.emerg                                          :omusrmsg:*

# Save news errors of level crit and higher in a special file.
uucp,news.crit                                   /var/log/spooler

# Save boot messages also to boot.log
local7.*                                         /var/log/boot.log


# ### sample forwarding rule ###
#action(type="omfwd"
# # An on-disk queue is created for this action. If the remote host is
```

This configuration directs various types of log messages to different files.
For instance, all kernel messages are sent to the console, while most informational
messages are written to */var/log/messages*. Security-related messages are stored in
/var/log/secure, and mail-related logs are kept in */var/log/maillog*.

To customize logging for specific applications or services, you can create
additional configuration files in the */etc/rsyslog.d* directory. These files are read by
rsyslog in alphabetical order, allowing for modular and organized logging
configurations.

Once you've configured your logging preferences, it's crucial to ensure that

the rsyslog service is running and set to start at boot time. You can do this using

systemctl:

sudo systemctl enable rsyslog

sudo systemctl start rsyslog

```
[root@zero2rhcsa-mrsa-com etc]# systemctl status rsyslog.service
* rsyslog.service - System Logging Service
     Loaded: loaded (/usr/lib/systemd/system/rsyslog.service; enabled; preset: enabled)
     Active: active (running) since Tue 2024-11-12 00:41:05 CST; 10h ago
       Docs: man:rsyslogd(8)
             https://www.rsyslog.com/doc/
   Main PID: 1450 (rsyslogd)
      Tasks: 3 (limit: 23030)
     Memory: 7.6M
        CPU: 4.246s
     CGroup: /system.slice/rsyslog.service
             └─1450 /usr/sbin/rsyslogd -n

Nov 12 00:41:04 zero2rhcsa-mrsa-com systemd[1]: Starting System Logging Service...
Nov 12 00:41:05 zero2rhcsa-mrsa-com rsyslogd[1450]: [origin software="rsyslogd" swVersion="8.2310.0-4.el9" x-pid="1450" x-info="https://www.rsyslog.com"]
Nov 12 00:41:05 zero2rhcsa-mrsa-com systemd[1]: Started System Logging Service.
Nov 12 00:41:06 zero2rhcsa-mrsa-com rsyslogd[1450]: imjournal: journal files changed, reloading... [v8.2310.0-4.el9 try https://www.rsyslog.com/e/0 ]
lines 1-16/16 (END)
```

With logging properly configured, we can now turn our attention to

analyzing log files. Log analysis is a critical skill for any Linux administrator, as it

allows you to troubleshoot issues, detect security threats, and gain insights into

system behavior.

One of the most commonly used tools for log analysis is the *'journalctl'*

command, which is part of the *systemd* suite. Journalctl provides a unified way to

query and display logs from all system components and services that use systemd's

logging features. Here are some useful *journalctl* commands:

View all log entries

journalctl

```
[root@zero2rhcsa-mrsa-com etc]# journalctl
Nov 12 00:46:32 zero2rhcsa kernel: Linux version 5.14.0-427.42.1.el9_4.x86_64 (mockbuild@x86-64-03.build.eng.rdu2.redhat.com) (gcc (GCC) 11.4.1 20231218
Nov 12 00:40:32 zero2rhcsa kernel: The list of certified hardware and cloud instances for Red Hat Enterprise Linux 9 can be viewed at the Red Hat Ecosyst
Nov 12 00:40:32 zero2rhcsa kernel: Command line: BOOT_IMAGE=(hd0,msdos2)/vmlinuz-5.14.0-427.42.1.el9_4.x86_64 root=/dev/mapper/rhel_vbox-root ro crashker
Nov 12 00:40:32 zero2rhcsa kernel: x86/fpu: x87 FPU will use FXSAVE
Nov 12 00:40:32 zero2rhcsa kernel: signal: max sigframe size: 1440
Nov 12 00:40:32 zero2rhcsa kernel: BIOS-provided physical RAM map:
Nov 12 00:40:32 zero2rhcsa kernel: BIOS-e820: [mem 0x0000000000000000-0x000000000009fbff] usable
Nov 12 00:40:32 zero2rhcsa kernel: BIOS-e820: [mem 0x000000000009fc00-0x000000000009ffff] reserved
Nov 12 00:40:32 zero2rhcsa kernel: BIOS-e820: [mem 0x00000000000f0000-0x00000000000fffff] reserved
```

View logs for a specific service

journalctl -u sshd.service

```
[root@zero2rhcsa-mrsa-com etc]# journalctl -u sshd.service
Nov 12 00:40:58 zero2rhcsa-mrsa-com systemd[1]: Starting OpenSSH server daemon...
Nov 12 00:40:59 zero2rhcsa-mrsa-com sshd[1202]: Server listening on 0.0.0.0 port 22.
Nov 12 00:40:59 zero2rhcsa-mrsa-com sshd[1202]: Server listening on :: port 22.
Nov 12 00:40:59 zero2rhcsa-mrsa-com systemd[1]: Started OpenSSH server daemon.
[root@zero2rhcsa-mrsa-com etc]#
```

View logs since the last boot

journalctl -b

```
[root@zero2rhcsa-mrsa-com etc]# journalctl -b
Nov 12 00:40:32 zero2rhcsa kernel: Linux version 5.14.0-427.42.1.el9_4.x86_64 (mockbuild@x86-64-03.build.eng.rdu2.redhat.com) (gcc (GCC) 11.4.1 20231218
Nov 12 00:40:32 zero2rhcsa kernel: The list of certified hardware and cloud instances for Red Hat Enterprise Linux 9 can be viewed at the Red Hat Ecosyst
Nov 12 00:40:32 zero2rhcsa kernel: Command line: BOOT_IMAGE=(hd0,msdos2)/vmlinuz-5.14.0-427.42.1.el9_4.x86_64 root=/dev/mapper/rhel_vbox-root ro crashker
Nov 12 00:40:32 zero2rhcsa kernel: x86/fpu: x87 FPU will use FXSAVE
Nov 12 00:40:32 zero2rhcsa kernel: signal: max sigframe size: 1440
Nov 12 00:40:32 zero2rhcsa kernel: BIOS-provided physical RAM map:
Nov 12 00:40:32 zero2rhcsa kernel: BIOS-e820: [mem 0x0000000000000000-0x000000000009fbff] usable
Nov 12 00:40:32 zero2rhcsa kernel: BIOS-e820: [mem 0x000000000009fc00-0x000000000009ffff] reserved
Nov 12 00:40:32 zero2rhcsa kernel: BIOS-e820: [mem 0x00000000000f0000-0x00000000000fffff] reserved
Nov 12 00:40:32 zero2rhcsa kernel: BIOS-e820: [mem 0x0000000000100000-0x00000000ddfeffff] usable
```

View logs from a specific time range

journalctl --since "2024-01-01 00:00:00" --until "2024-01-02 00:00:00"

View logs in real-time

journalctl -f

```
[root@zero2rhcsa-mrsa-com etc]# journalctl -f
Nov 12 11:11:52 zero2rhcsa-mrsa-com systemd[1]: Starting Network Manager Script Dispatcher Service...
Nov 12 11:11:52 zero2rhcsa-mrsa-com systemd[1]: Started Network Manager Script Dispatcher Service.
Nov 12 11:12:02 zero2rhcsa-mrsa-com systemd[1]: NetworkManager-dispatcher.service: Deactivated successfully.
Nov 12 11:16:52 zero2rhcsa-mrsa-com NetworkManager[1165]: <info>  [1731431812.5307] dhcp4 (enp0s8): state changed new lease, address=192.168.56.101
Nov 12 11:16:52 zero2rhcsa-mrsa-com systemd[1]: Starting Network Manager Script Dispatcher Service...
Nov 12 11:16:52 zero2rhcsa-mrsa-com systemd[1]: Started Network Manager Script Dispatcher Service.
Nov 12 11:17:02 zero2rhcsa-mrsa-com systemd[1]: NetworkManager-dispatcher.service: Deactivated successfully.
Nov 12 11:20:04 zero2rhcsa-mrsa-com systemd[1]: Starting system activity accounting tool...
Nov 12 11:20:04 zero2rhcsa-mrsa-com systemd[1]: sysstat-collect.service: Deactivated successfully.
Nov 12 11:20:04 zero2rhcsa-mrsa-com systemd[1]: Finished system activity accounting tool.
Nov 13 11:21:53 zero2rhcsa-mrsa-com NetworkManager[1165]: <info>  [1731432112.5332] dhcp4 (enp0s8): state changed new lease, address=192.168.56.101
Nov 12 11:21:52 zero2rhcsa-mrsa-com systemd[1]: Starting Network Manager Script Dispatcher Service...
Nov 12 11:21:52 zero2rhcsa-mrsa-com systemd[1]: Started Network Manager Script Dispatcher Service.
Nov 12 11:22:02 zero2rhcsa-mrsa-com systemd[1]: NetworkManager-dispatcher.service: Deactivated successfully.
```

For more traditional log files stored in */var/log/*, tools like *'grep'*, *'awk'*, and *'sed'* are invaluable for extracting relevant information. For example, to search for failed login attempts in the secure log:

grep "gkr-pam" /var/log/secure

```
[root@zero2rhcsa-mrsa-com etc]# grep "gkr-pam" /var/log/secure
Nov 10 01:42:17 zero2rhcsa-mrsa-com gdm-password][9201]: gkr-pam: unable to locate daemon control file
Nov 10 01:42:17 zero2rhcsa-mrsa-com gdm-password][9291]: gkr-pam: stashed password to try later in open session
Nov 10 01:42:17 zero2rhcsa-mrsa-com gdm-password][9291]: gkr-pam: gnome-keyring-daemon started properly and unlocked keyring
Nov 10 10:00:30 zero2rhcsa-mrsa-com gdm-password][4481]: gkr-pam: unable to locate daemon control file
Nov 10 10:06:36 zero2rhcsa-mrsa-com gdm-password][4481]: gkr-pam: stashed password to try later in open session
Nov 10 10:06:39 zero2rhcsa-mrsa-com gdm-password][4481]: gkr-pam: gnome-keyring-daemon started properly and unlocked keyring
Nov 10 10:16:11 zero2rhcsa-mrsa-com gdm-password][3699]: gkr-pam: unable to locate daemon control file
Nov 10 10:16:11 zero2rhcsa-mrsa-com gdm-password][3699]: gkr-pam: stashed password to try later in open session
Nov 10 10:16:11 zero2rhcsa-mrsa-com gdm-password][3699]: gkr-pam: gnome-keyring-daemon started properly and unlocked keyring
Nov 11 09:22:54 zero2rhcsa-mrsa-com gdm-password][6206]: gkr-pam: unable to locate daemon control file
Nov 11 09:22:54 zero2rhcsa-mrsa-com gdm-password][6206]: gkr-pam: stashed password to try later in open session
Nov 11 09:22:54 zero2rhcsa-mrsa-com gdm-password][6206]: gkr-pam: gnome-keyring-daemon started properly and unlocked keyring
Nov 11 10:44:17 zero2rhcsa-mrsa-com gdm-password][4555]: gkr-pam: unable to locate daemon control file
Nov 11 10:44:17 zero2rhcsa-mrsa-com gdm-password][4555]: gkr-pam: stashed password to try later in open session
Nov 11 10:44:18 zero2rhcsa-mrsa-com gdm-password][4555]: gkr-pam: gnome-keyring-daemon started properly and unlocked keyring
Nov 11 17:11:17 zero2rhcsa-mrsa-com gdm-password][1831L]: gkr-pam: unlocked login keyring
Nov 12 00:44:23 zero2rhcsa-mrsa-com gdm-password][6731]: gkr-pam: unable to locate daemon control file
Nov 12 00:44:23 zero2rhcsa-mrsa-com gdm-password][6731]: gkr-pam: stashed password to try later in open session
Nov 12 00:44:24 zero2rhcsa-mrsa-com gdm-password][6731]: gkr-pam: gnome-keyring-daemon started properly and unlocked keyring
[root@zero2rhcsa-mrsa-com etc]#
```

As you become more proficient in log analysis, you may want to explore more advanced tools like *'logwatch'* or *'goaccess'*, which can provide summarized reports and visualizations of log data.

Moving beyond logging, monitoring system performance is crucial for maintaining the health and efficiency of your Linux systems. There are numerous tools available for this purpose, each offering unique insights into different aspects of system performance.

One of the most versatile monitoring tools is *'top'*, which provides a real-time, dynamic view of system processes. When you run *'top'*, you'll see output similar to this:

This output provides a wealth of information, including CPU usage, memory utilization, and details about individual processes. The *'htop'* command offers a more user-friendly and colorful interface with similar functionality.

For monitoring disk usage, the 'df' and 'du' commands are indispensable. *'df'*

shows disk space usage for mounted file systems:

```
[root@zero2rhcsa-mrsa-com ~]# df -h
Filesystem                    Size  Used Avail Use% Mounted on
devtmpfs                      4.0M     0  4.0M   0% /dev
tmpfs                         1.8G     0  1.8G   0% /dev/shm
tmpfs                         732M   15M  718M   2% /run
/dev/mapper/rhel_vbox-root     25G  8.5G   17G  35% /
/dev/sda2                     1.8G  512M  7.5G  18% /boot
/dev/mapper/rhel_vbox-var      15G  7.2G   14G   8% /var
/dev/mapper/rhel_vbox-home     20G  984M   19G   5% /home
tmpfs                         366M  164K  366M   1% /run/user/1000
[root@zero2rhcsa-mrsa-com ~]#
```

'du' is useful for determining the size of specific directories:

du -sh /home/*

```
[root@zero2rhcsa-mrsa-com ~]# du -sh /home/*
884M    /home/obert
[root@zero2rhcsa-mrsa-com ~]#
```

To monitor network activity, tools like *'netstat'*, *'ss'*, and *'iftop'* can provide

valuable insights. For instance, *'netstat -tuln'* will show all listening TCP and UDP

ports:

netstat -tuln

```
[root@zero2rhcsa-mrsa-com ~]# netstat -tuln
Active Internet connections (only servers)
Proto Recv-Q Send-Q Local Address           Foreign Address         State
tcp        0      0 0.0.0.0:111             0.0.0.0:*               LISTEN
tcp        0      0 127.0.0.1:44321         0.0.0.0:*               LISTEN
tcp        0      0 0.0.0.0:22              0.0.0.0:*               LISTEN
tcp        0      0 127.0.0.1:6430          0.0.0.0:*               LISTEN
tcp        0      0 127.0.0.1:631           0.0.0.0:*               LISTEN
tcp6       0      0 :::631                  :::*                    LISTEN
tcp6       0      0 :::111                  :::*                    LISTEN
tcp6       0      0 :::22                   :::*                    LISTEN
tcp6       0      0 :::6430                 :::*                    LISTEN
tcp6       0      0 :::44321                :::*                    LISTEN
udp        0      0 0.0.0.0:39646           0.0.0.0:*
udp        0      0 0.0.0.0:5353            0.0.0.0:*
udp        0      0 0.0.0.0:111             0.0.0.0:*
udp        0      0 127.0.0.1:323           0.0.0.0:*
udp6       0      0 :::5353                 :::*
udp6       0      0 :::111                  :::*
udp6       0      0 :::35302                :::*
udp6       0      0 fe80::1a00:27ff:fe3f:546 :::*
[root@zero2rhcsa-mrsa-com ~]#
```

For more comprehensive system monitoring, consider using tools like 'Nagios', 'Zabbix', or 'Prometheus', which offer advanced features such as alerting, graphing, and distributed monitoring capabilities.

An often overlooked but crucial aspect of system administration is the creation and management of cron jobs. Cron is a time-based job scheduler in Unix-like operating systems, allowing users to schedule jobs (commands or shell scripts) to run periodically at fixed times, dates, or intervals.

To create a cron job, you typically use the '*crontab*' command. Each user can have their own crontab file, and there's also a system-wide crontab. To edit your personal crontab:

crontab -e

This will open your default text editor. The syntax for a cron job is as follows:

* * * * * command_to_execute

The five asterisks mean the following, respectively:

minute (0-59),

hour (0-23),

day of month (1-31),

month (1-12), and

day of the week (0-7, 0 and 7 represent Sunday).

For example, to run a backup script every day at 3:30 AM:

30 3 * * * /path/to/backup_script.sh

To run a script every 15 minutes:

*/15 * * * * /path/to/script.sh

Remember to use absolute paths in your cron jobs, as the working directory and environment variables may not be what you expect when the job runs.

It's also important to manage the output of your cron jobs. By default, cron will email the output to the user who owns the crontab. If you don't want this behavior, you can redirect output to a file or to /dev/null:

30 2 * * * /path/to/backup_script.sh > /var/log/backup.log 2>&1

This redirects both standard output and standard error to a log file.

As we conclude this chapter on system monitoring and logging, it's worth emphasizing the importance of these practices in maintaining a healthy and secure

Linux environment. Effective monitoring and logging not only help in troubleshooting issues but also play a crucial role in detecting and preventing security breaches. As you continue to hone your skills as a Linux administrator, remember that the ability to effectively monitor your systems and interpret log data is just as important as knowing how to configure and maintain them.

In the next chapter, we'll explore the critical topics of backup, recovery, and system maintenance. These practices are essential for ensuring the continuity and reliability of your Linux systems, complementing the monitoring and logging skills you've acquired in this chapter. We'll delve into strategies for creating robust backup solutions, techniques for system recovery, and best practices for ongoing system maintenance, including updating and patching your systems to keep them secure and up-to-date.

Chapter 10:

Backup, Recovery, and System Maintenance

As we transition from monitoring and logging our Linux systems, we now turn our attention to the critical aspects of backup, recovery, and system maintenance. These processes are fundamental to ensuring the longevity, reliability, and security of any Linux environment, particularly in enterprise settings where data integrity and system uptime are paramount.

Implementing backup strategies is the first line of defense against data loss and system failures. In the world of Linux administration, backups are not merely a precautionary measure; they are an essential component of responsible system management. A well-designed backup strategy can mean the difference between a minor inconvenience and a catastrophic data loss event.

When considering backup strategies, it's crucial to understand the different types of backups available. Full backups, as the name suggests, involve copying all data from a system or specific directories. While comprehensive, full backups can be time-consuming and resource-intensive. Incremental backups, on the other hand, only copy data that has changed since the last backup, offering a more efficient approach for regular backups.

One popular tool for creating backups in Linux systems is '*rsync*'. This versatile utility allows for efficient file synchronization and can be used to create both local and remote backups. A typical *rsync* command for creating a backup might look like this:

rsync -avz /source/directory /destination/directory... but it is advisable adding options like -avh to enhance the command for backup purposes. For example:

Here, '*-a*' preserves the attributes of the files, '*-v*' provides verbose output, and '*-z*' compresses the data during transfer. This command structure forms the basis of many backup scripts used in production environments.

Another powerful backup tool is '*tar*', which can create compressed archive files of entire directory structures. A common tar command for creating a backup might be:

tar -czvf backup.tar.gz /directory/to/backup

In this command, '*-c*' creates a new archive, '*-z*' compresses the archive with gzip, '*-v*' provides verbose output, and '*-f*' specifies the filename of the archive.

When implementing a backup strategy, it's crucial to consider the "3-2-1" rule. This rule suggests keeping at least three copies of your data, stored on two different types of media, with one copy kept off-site. This approach provides redundancy and protects against various failure scenarios, from hardware malfunctions to natural disasters.

Scheduling regular backups is as important as the backup process itself. The 'cron' utility, which we explored in the previous chapter, is an excellent tool for automating backup tasks. A typical cron job for daily backups might look like this:

*0 1 * * * /path/to/backup/script.sh. For example:*

*0 3 * * * /home/obert/scripts_dir/pkg_index_update.sh*

This cron job would run the backup script every day at 1:00 AM, while the second will update the dnf/yum package index every day at 3:00 AM.

While creating backups is crucial, the ability to restore from these backups is equally important. Restoration procedures should be thoroughly tested to ensure that backups are not only being created but are also viable for recovery purposes. Regular restore tests should be part of any comprehensive backup strategy.

The '*tar*' command we used earlier for creating backups can also be used for restoration. To extract files from a tar archive, you would use:

tar -xzvf backup.tar.gz -C /destination/directory

Here, '*-x*' extracts files from the archive, and '*-C*' specifies the directory where the files should be extracted.

For more complex restoration scenarios, particularly those involving system-wide backups, tools like '*dd*' can be invaluable. The '*dd*' command can create and restore exact copies of entire disk partitions or drives. However, it should be used with caution as incorrect usage can lead to data loss.

Moving beyond backups and restoration, system maintenance is another critical aspect of Linux administration. Regular system updates and patches are essential for maintaining the security and stability of your Linux systems. In Red

Hat Enterprise Linux (RHEL), the primary tool for managing updates is *'yum'* (or *'dnf'* in more recent versions).

To check for available updates, you would use:

sudo yum check-update

```
[root@zero2rhcsa-mrsa-com ~]# yum check-update
Updating Subscription Management repositories.
Last metadata expiration check: 2:28:38 ago on Wed 13 Nov 2024 11:13:03 AM CST.

NetworkManager-libreswan.x86_64                    1.2.22-4.el9_5           rhel-9-for-x86_64-appstream-rpms
expat.x86_64                                       2.5.0-3.el9_5.1          rhel-9-for-x86_64-baseos-rpms
firefox.x86_64                                     128.4.0-1.el9_5          rhel-9-for-x86_64-appstream-rpms
libsoup.x86_64                                     2.72.0-8.el9_5.2         rhel-9-for-x86_64-appstream-rpms
webkit2gtk3.x86_64                                 2.46.3-1.el9_5.2         rhel-9-for-x86_64-appstream-rpms
webkit2gtk3-jsc.x86_64                             2.46.3-1.el9_5           rhel-9-for-x86_64-appstream-rpms
[root@zero2rhcsa-mrsa-com ~]#
```

To apply all available updates:

sudo yum update

```
[root@zero2rhcsa-mrsa-com ~]# yum update
Updating Subscription Management repositories.
Last metadata expiration check: 2:29:34 ago on Wed 13 Nov 2024 11:13:03 AM CST.
Dependencies resolved.
=======================================================================================================================
 Package                    Architecture      Version               Repository                              Size
=======================================================================================================================
Upgrading:
 NetworkManager-libreswan   x86_64            1.2.22-4.el9_5        rhel-9-for-x86_64-appstream-rpms        165 k
 expat                      x86_64            2.5.0-3.el9_5.1       rhel-9-for-x86_64-baseos-rpms           119 k
 firefox                    x86_64            128.4.0-1.el9_5       rhel-9-for-x86_64-appstream-rpms        123 M
 libsoup                    x86_64            2.72.0-8.el9_5.2      rhel-9-for-x86_64-appstream-rpms        407 k
 webkit2gtk3                x86_64            2.46.3-1.el9_5        rhel-9-for-x86_64-appstream-rpms         25 M
 webkit2gtk3-jsc            x86_64            2.46.3-1.el9_5        rhel-9-for-x86_64-appstream-rpms        4.4 M

Transaction Summary
=======================================================================================================================
Upgrade  6 Packages

Total download size: 153 M
Is this ok [y/N]: y
Downloading Packages:
(1/6): NetworkManager-libreswan-1.2.22-4.el9_5.x86_64.rpm                                447 kB/s | 165 kB     00:00
(2/6): webkit2gtk3-2.46.3-1.el9_5.x86_64.rpm                                              13 MB/s |  25 MB     00:02
(3/6): firefox-128.4.0-1.el9_5.x86_64.rpm                                                 36 MB/s | 123 MB     00:03
(4/6): webkit2gtk3-jsc-2.46.3-1.el9_5.x86_64.rpm                                         5.5 MB/s | 4.4 MB     00:00
(5/6): expat-2.5.0-3.el9_5.1.x86_64.rpm                                                  377 kB/s | 119 kB     00:00
[MIRROR] libsoup-2.72.0-8.el9_5.2.x86_64.rpm: Curl error (28): Timeout was reached for https://cdn.redhat.com/content/dist/rhel9/9/x86_64/appstream/os/Packa
ges/l/libsoup-2.72.0-8.el9_5.2.x86_64.rpm [Operation timed out after 30000 milliseconds with 0 out of 0 bytes received]
(6/6): libsoup-2.72.0-8.el9_5.2.x86_64.rpm                                                13 kB/s | 407 kB     00:30
-----------------------------------------------------------------------------------------------------------------------
Total                                                                                    5.0 MB/s | 153 MB     00:30
Running transaction check
Transaction check succeeded.
Running transaction test
Transaction test succeeded.
```

It's important to note that while keeping systems up-to-date is crucial, updates should be applied judiciously, especially in production environments. It's often advisable to test updates in a non-production environment before applying them to critical systems.

In addition to software updates, regular system maintenance should include tasks such as checking disk usage, monitoring system logs for unusual activity, and verifying the integrity of important system files. The '*df*' command is useful for checking disk usage:

df -h

The '*-h*' option provides human-readable output.

For monitoring system logs, tools like '*journalctl*' (for systems using *systemd*) or traditional log files in '*/var/log/*' can provide valuable insights into system health and potential issues.

Another crucial aspect of system maintenance is managing boot issues. Understanding the boot process and being able to troubleshoot boot problems is an essential skill for any Linux administrator. The boot process in modern Linux systems typically involves several stages, including the BIOS/UEFI, bootloader (usually GRUB2 in RHEL), kernel initialization, and system initialization (managed by systemd in RHEL).

When troubleshooting boot issues, the ability to boot into single-user mode or rescue mode can be invaluable. To enter single-user mode in GRUB2, you would edit the kernel command line and add '*single*' or '*rd.break*' at the end. This allows you to perform maintenance tasks or fix issues that prevent normal system boot.

For more severe issues where the system won't boot at all, you might need to use a rescue disk or live CD. RHEL provides rescue mode options in its installation media, allowing you to mount the system's root filesystem and perform repairs.

One common boot issue is a corrupted or missing GRUB configuration. In such cases, you may need to reinstall or reconfigure GRUB. This can typically be done from a rescue environment using commands like:

grub2-install /dev/sda

grub2-mkconfig -o /boot/grub2/grub.cfg

These commands reinstall GRUB to the master boot record of the first hard drive and regenerate the GRUB configuration file, respectively.

Another aspect of system maintenance that shouldn't be overlooked is performance tuning. While RHEL comes with sensible defaults, there may be times when you need to optimize your system for specific workloads. This could involve adjusting kernel parameters via the '/etc/sysctl.conf' file, optimizing file system choices and mount options, or fine-tuning resource limits in '/etc/security/limits.conf'.

For example, to improve network performance for high-traffic servers, you might adjust some network-related kernel parameters:

net.core.somaxconn = 1024

net.core.netdev_max_backlog = 5000

net.ipv4.tcp_max_syn_backlog = 8096

These parameters would be added to '*/etc/sysctl.conf*' and applied with the '*sysctl -p*' command.

It's worth noting that performance tuning is often a process of careful measurement, adjustment, and re-measurement. Tools like 'top', *'iostat'*, and *'sar'* can provide valuable insights into system performance and help guide your tuning efforts.

As we conclude this chapter on backup, recovery, and system maintenance, it's important to emphasize that these processes are not one-time tasks, but ongoing responsibilities of a Linux administrator. Regular backups, diligent system updates, and proactive maintenance are key to ensuring the stability, security, and longevity of your Linux systems.

Going from a Linux noobie to the Red Hat Certified System Administrator (RHCSA) certification is likely one of the most useful things that you can do in your career. In this book, you have started with foolproof concepts, practical hands-on exercises, and completed complex administrative tasks to boost your confidence along with your technical skill set. Linux mastery is not an exam but a lifelong skill set that equips you to solve real-world problems. It helps you enhance systems and grow your career in the constantly changing IT realm!

But on your journey of Linux, remember, expertise is earned by practicing continuously—keep your mind open and never hesitate to take challenges. Now that you have this knowledge, your career can progress in so many ways: an open-source contribution; a deeper understanding of system administration. So, continue to experiment and learn as you stretch what your talent can do. You have just started your Linux journey, and skills learned here will be the foundation of so much more.

Appendices

Appendices A:

Linux Commands Reference

A quick-reference table for essential Linux commands that are covered throughout the book, categorized for easy lookup.

Commands	Description	Example Usages
systemctl	Manages systemd services	systemctl restart sshd
ps	Displays currently running processes	ps aux
chown	Changes file ownership	chown user:group abc.txt
chmod	Changes file permissions	chmod 755 abc.txt
cd	Changes the current directory	cd /etc
ls	Lists directory contents	ls -l /var/log

Appendix B:

Key Configuration Files

An overview of important Linux configuration files is discussed in the book.

File Path	Purpose	Example configurations

/etc/hosts	Static hostname resolution	Locally maps hostnames to IPs.
/etc/fstab	File systems and mount points	Specifies file systems to be mounted at boot
/etc/group	Group account information	For user group management
/etc/passwd	User account information	Format: username:x:UID:GID:info:home:shell

Appendix C:

RHCSA Exam Preparation Tips

Key advice and strategies for preparing for the RHCSA exam.

- ❖ **Hands-on Practice**: Spend ample time working in a test environment to practice each skill outlined in the RHCSA objectives.
- ❖ **Time Management**: Learn how to balance time effectively during the exam by practicing simulated test scenarios.
- ❖ **Review Man Pages**: Familiarize yourself with the man (manual) pages for detailed command usage and options.

Appendix D:

Useful Online Resources

A curated list of helpful websites and resources for Linux administrators and RHCSA candidates.

- ❖ **Official Red Hat Documentation**: Comprehensive guides and documentation for RHEL [*link: https://access.redhat.com/documentation/*].
- ❖ **Linux Command Library**: A collection of common Linux commands and examples [*link: https://linuxcommandlibrary.com/*].
- ❖ **GitHub Repositories**: Open-source scripts and tools for practice and

  study.

Appendix E:

Troubleshooting Checklist

Common troubleshooting scenarios with suggested solutions.

- ❖ **System Won't Boot**: Check the GRUB configuration and ensure the root file system is intact.
- ❖ **Network Issues**: Verify the network interface configuration using *ip addr* show and review */etc/resolv.conf* for DNS issues.
- ❖ **Permission Denied Errors**: Use ls -l to check file permissions and chmod/chown to adjust as needed.

Appendix F:

Glossary of Terms

Definitions for key technical terms used throughout the book.

- ❖ **Kernel**: The core component of the operating system, managing hardware and system processes.
- ❖ **Daemon**: A background service running without direct user interaction.
- ❖ **LVM (Logical Volume Management)**: A system for managing disk storage that allows flexible partitioning.

Appendix G:

Command-Line Shortcuts and Tips

Efficiency tips for using the Linux command line.

- ❖ **Tab Completion**: Use Tab to auto-complete file paths and commands.
- ❖ **Ctrl + R**: Search command history interactively.
- ❖ **Aliases**: Create shortcuts for long commands, e.g., alias *ll='ls -la'*.